Praise for *Elvis: The Army Years Uncovered*

"The way Trina Young tells the story in easy to understand language from beginning to end and the extensive research that supports it at every step, make *Elvis: The Army Years Uncovered* the best account to date of Elvis Presley's life during his years of military service."

Alan Hanson, author,
Elvis '57: The Final Fifties Tours

Trina Young "has an entertaining and colorful writing style... she wrote a knowledgeable and easy to read book... adding new elements and perspectives on these two years. Young stayed away from the 'what-ifs' but handed the reader the material to make up his/her own mind."

Kees Mouwen, author
Elvis Day by Day

Also by the Author

ELVIS: Behind The Legend:
Startling Truths About The King of Rock and Roll's
Life, Loves, Films and Music

Elvis and The Beatles:
Love and Rivalry Between the
Two Biggest Acts of the 20th Century

ELVIS
THE ARMY YEARS
UNCOVERED

Behind the Scenes of
the Two Years that Changed
The King of Rock and Roll's life

TRINA YOUNG

ELVIS: THE ARMY YEARS UNCOVERED
Behind the Scenes of
the Two Years that Changed
The King of Rock and Roll's Life

Copyright © 2021 by Trina Yannicos

Cover photo: U.S. Army (3/60)
[This image was cropped and the white background was
removed to emphasize the subject.]

Disclaimer: The appearance of U.S. Department of Defense (DoD)
visual information does not imply or constitute DoD endorsement.

Back cover:
Elvis jacket: Trina Young
Author photo: Kevin Thomas

ISBN: 979-8549856943

Dedicated to:

Joan and Paul Gansky

CONTENTS

INTRODUCTION

"I would like to write a book about my Army experience."
Elvis Presley

The world got all shook up when The King of Rock and Roll had to put his career on hold to serve two years in the U.S. Army. From March 1958 to March 1960, Elvis Presley's movie career was forcibly stalled and so was his recording career. As a result, with Elvis out of show business at the height of his fame, history over the years has disregarded these two years in Presley's life as mostly uneventful.

On the contrary, the 24 months that Elvis spent in the army would alter the star's life in so many ways. As friend Jerry Schilling put it: "He [Elvis] went in as James Dean and came out as John Wayne."

But that is much too simple a statement to summarize those two life-changing years which would redefine, reshape and revamp the life and career of Elvis Aaron Presley. While behind the scenes, Elvis thought being drafted was the worst thing that could have happened to him, in some ways it turned out to be the best.

Therefore, it is not surprising that even with the unprecedented amount of news coverage Presley got during these two years, Elvis himself still felt that he had much more to say about his experience as a soldier. Upon his release in March 1960, Elvis told reporters that he wanted to write a book about it someday.

Unfortunately, Elvis never wrote his book, but we wish he had. Because, in truth, the American press did not know about everything that went on with Elvis in Germany. Not every story and tidbit about Elvis made it back to the States, leaving many details undocumented. That is why Presley's time as a soldier appears to be the most exciting and yet most mysterious period during The King of Rock and Roll's life and career.

Most Elvis fans know the superficial story of Presley's army years - the public relations version. But with hindsight and over 60 years of accumulating eyewitness accounts, it is now time to go behind the scenes in the life of the most famous U.S. army soldier of all time. A journey into the life of Private Presley, who rose to the rank of Sergeant, includes the stories of many women, nightclubs, strippers, death rumors, secret concerts and fan encounters to name a few.

Many biographical accounts of Presley's life seem to quickly skim through the "army years." These narratives unknowingly omit captivating stories about Elvis ranging from the most raucous to the most warm-hearted. In *ELVIS: The Army Years Uncovered*, many aspects of Presley's time in the army that were never reported or never made it into the history books are now revealed.

Fascinating untold stories have been coming out over the years involving the highs and lows Presley experienced as a soldier away from the public eye. A more frightening episode that was kept from the press was the fact that Elvis almost died during maneuvers.

While scouting an area one night in Germany in their jeep, Elvis and his sergeant pulled over onto the side of the road to sleep. Elvis kept the engine running with the heater on since it was so cold. Presley and his sergeant pulled their ponchos over their heads to keep the cold wind off them, and then they both fell asleep. However, as the gas fumes from the jeep started creeping under the ponchos, both Elvis and his sergeant became unconscious.

"The next thing I knew, the wind blew one corner of my poncho away from my face," Elvis told army buddy Charlie Hodge. "The fresh air woke me up some... I was too sick and weak to even raise my hands... So I tried to tilt myself over and just fall out of the Jeep. I fell face down in the snow and got sick all over the place."

Elvis was showing signs of carbon monoxide poisoning. If Elvis had not regained consciousness, he and his sergeant most likely would have died from the poisonous carbon monoxide fumes. Imagine The King of Rock and Roll dying so senselessly in a stroke of bad luck.

"While Elvis and the Sergeant were lying there unconscious, a really strong wind came and blew the tarp off the jeep," explained Presley's friend, Joe Esposito. "That's what saved their lives. That really happened... Talk about divine intervention."

After being jolted to wake up, Elvis looked over at his sergeant who appeared "stiff" with his head down. "He looked dead," Elvis said. Presley nudged his sergeant who then fell out of the jeep on the passenger's side. Elvis helped him get on his feet as the sergeant regained consciousness. After regaining their composure, Elvis and his sergeant got back into the vehicle and left. They decided not to mention it to anyone in the army since the incident could get them both into trouble – not to mention it would be a public relations nightmare.

"That one was real close," Elvis told his friends. "Real close."

This incident is just one example of the many surprising facts and revelations about the two hidden years in the life of Private Presley. Many of these behind-the-scenes events were things that Presley's manager, Colonel Parker, would never have wanted to be exposed to the public.

In fact, most people do not realize how much danger Presley and his fellow soldiers were in. The Cold War could have quickly escalated into a land war due to tensions at the border between East Germany supported by the Soviet Union and West Germany supported by the U.S.

"It was more like war than you might think," Presley's fellow soldier, Rex Mansfield said. "It was not peacetime. It was 'be ready' time... We'd been warned [war with Russia] could happen at any time."

Luckily, Presley never had to participate in combat during those two years, but that does not mean it was not high-risk, as Lieutenant William J. Taylor explained: "I simply cannot forget the fact that Elvis chose to serve in a combat unit... Aside from the fact that our battalion could have gone to war with the Soviets at any time, there are real risks every single training day in a combat unit. I have seen a tank loader's head smashed by a 90 mm main gun recoil, hands mutilated or cut off by engine maintenance accidents, an eye put out by blank ammo fired in someone's face, a soldier's body crushed by a tank rolling over it, a leg smashed behind a jeep with a stuck accelerator pedal, horrible burns from fuel accidents – I could go on."

Instead of helping Elvis avoid service or get a cushy assignment, The Colonel saw to it that his client would make the best of the situation with the image that Presley would serve just like any other soldier. And Parker made sure the public knew that by taking every opportunity to get publicity for his client, especially during the first six months Elvis was serving in the States.

The media circus began in March 1958 during Presley's induction. Reporters documented nearly every step that Presley took during those first few days of transitioning from civilian to serviceman.

Photographers followed Elvis everywhere from his swearing in, to his medical exam, to getting fitted for his army uniform, and getting his jaw-dropping G.I. haircut. Presley's induction made news around the country with headlines like "Elvis Presley Swaps Guitar for Army Rifle" and "It's Drill, Bugles for Elvis as Army Halts Rock 'n' Roll."

Six months later, in September 1958, when Elvis left for his new assignment in Germany, Parker was also on-hand to maximize the media attention. But once his client stepped onto German soil on October 1, 1958, Parker's power over Presley's personal life would be minimized for the next 17 months since he would remain in the U.S. without ever visiting Elvis in Germany.

However, the public interest in Elvis did not stop once he left America. The Associated Press and United Press International were distributing their stories from Germany about Presley's life as a soldier to the newspapers in the U.S. As a result, Elvis was constantly making the U.S. newspaper headlines during his time in Germany throughout late 1958, 1959 and early 1960 until he left in March.

Even though Elvis was being scrutinized in Germany not only by the press, but also by the fans, Presley was still able to keep his personal life private. Ironically, even though Elvis was confined to army life during the day, at night and on the weekends, he experienced the most freedom he would ever have for the rest of his life.

The 17 months out of the U.S. public spotlight offered Elvis a time to live like a normal person again, to a degree. In fact, since becoming a household name in 1956, this would be the only time in the remainder of Presley's career until his death in 1977 that Colonel Parker would not be there to exert management control over his client.

"I believe that the months spent in Germany were some of the happiest times in the life of the star," observed a German reporter who Presley befriended. "His private life was comparatively undisturbed. He wasn't on the run from one appointment to another and he wasn't under the constant pressure of success."

In his own words, Elvis summed it up best at a welcome home press conference on March 3, 1960 – the day he returned to American soil. When a reporter asked Presley if "sobering army life" changed his mind about rock and roll, Elvis could not help but chuckle at the question.

"Sobering army life..." Elvis repeated, as he rubbed his chin in thought. "Uh, no, it hasn't. It hasn't changed my mind because I was in tanks for a long time, you see, and they rock and roll quite a bit."

Knowing all the behind-the-scenes escapades that Elvis experienced for 17 months in Germany, one could read between the lines of Presley's seemingly innocent, yet very telling response. The truth is the King of Rock and Roll's time in the army was anything but "sobering."

Trina Young

1

THE ELVIS ARMY BACKLASH

From Elvis Presley's perspective, being drafted at the height of his entertainment career in 1958 was one of the worst things that could have happened to him. And his fans agreed.

The news had been brewing for over a year since January 4, 1957 when Elvis reported for his pre-induction physical at Kennedy Veterans Hospital in Memphis. A few days later on Presley's 22nd birthday, the Memphis Draft Board announced that Elvis had been classified as 1-A: available for unrestricted military service. This meant Presley was eligible to be drafted into any branch of the military. Fans started to panic wondering when the official word would come that their hero, The King of Rock and Roll, would be called to duty.

There was a huge public outcry to the news that the biggest recording star of the day would be drafted. The shock and dismay of the fans was expressed in several novelty songs which were released before and during Presley's stint in the army. Elvis' impending military service even inspired an award-winning 1960 Broadway musical, *Bye Bye Birdie*, which then became adapted into a film in 1963.

However, even those who were not Elvis fans were upset about Presley's impending military service because of the false perception that Elvis would get special treatment. Reports spread that Elvis would not have to cut his hair or get rid of his sideburns. Indignant parents and even congressmen complained that Elvis should not get off easy compared to the other young men his age by serving as an entertainer. The army was embarrassed by these stories and released a statement that there had been no plan for Elvis to get any preferential treatment.

In March 1957, Elvis was interviewed about his impending draft on the set of *Jailhouse Rock*: "I'm not worried about my hair or sideburns... I don't expect any special privileges or favors. Those people in the service are fair. They demand discipline and respect. And that's what I'll give 'em."

News finally came out on December 16, 1957 that Presley's draft status was "hot" – meaning he would soon receive his induction notice. Ironically, Milton Bowers, Sr., Chairman of the Memphis Draft Board, did not want to send Presley's notice through the mail and take a chance of the news getting out, so he wrote Elvis a letter requesting that he come see him in person. On December 20, Elvis complied and Bowers handed him his "greetings" from Uncle Sam. He was to report for duty on January 20, 1958.

When Elvis got his induction notice in December 1957, it was reported that the Army, Navy and Air Force were all fighting over who would get the new recruit. These branches of the military were all offering Elvis "special" treatment.

Presley's friend, George Klein, described an offer from the Air Force where Elvis would be treated like a military VIP working primarily as a public relations officer "touring Air Force bases to keep morale high." Klein pointed out the one little problem with that offer: "Elvis doesn't like to fly."

Meanwhile, the Navy proposed an "Elvis Presley Company" that could be specially trained and filled with Presley's friends from Memphis. Perks would allow for Elvis to perform in Las Vegas and be provided special VIP quarters. The Army made Presley an offer of "first-class tours of bases all over the world" to boost morale and encourage enlistment. The cushy assignment of entertaining troops was referred to in the military as "the celebrity wimp-out."

Ginger Alden, Presley's fiancée at the time of his death, documented in her book that her father, Sgt. Walter Alden, who was an army recruiter in Memphis at the time, personally attempted to advise Elvis on behalf of the army to voluntarily enlist in order to be eligible for "special opportunities." However, Alden was told that Elvis "had decided not to enlist and would take his chances with the draft."

The Colonel knew it would look bad if Elvis got off easier because he was a celebrity. In fact, sentiment had been brewing throughout 1957 in the media about the perception that Presley would get off easy due to his celebrity status: "It must be a nice thought to a draftee to think about the ease with which Presley is paying his obligation while they are marching blisters on heels, lackying for brass, mess cleaning or any one of hundreds of other very distasteful things in the Army," wrote one columnist.

As a result, Colonel Parker advised Elvis to turn down all of these "special" offers: "You gotta go in as a line soldier just like a regular guy, serve as any other recruit, and come home a hero," Colonel Parker said convincingly to Elvis. "Taking any of these deals will make millions of Americans angry."

In February 1958, one month before his military induction, a song "Bye Bye Elvis" by teenager Genee Harris was released. The song was one of several that expressed the despair felt by Presley's fans around the world about Elvis entering the army. It was followed by another song called "Dear 53310761" by The Threeteens released in May 1958 which affectionately referred to Presley by his army serial number.

Fans became so desperate that they started writing to the draft board and even President Eisenhower in hopes of getting Elvis relieved of his army duties. For example, right after Presley got inducted, a letter was sent in April 1958 to First Lady Mamie Eisenhower asking for Elvis to be released:

"Dear Mamie,

Will you please please be so sweet and kind as to ask Ike to please bring Elvis Presley back to us from the Army. We need him in our entertainment world to make us all laugh. The theatres need him to help fill their many empty seats these days of TV. Elvis is the leading box office attraction. Also did you know Elvis has been paying $500,000 in income taxes. We feel the huge taxes he has been paying could help our defense effort far more than his stay in the Army. Please ask Ike to bring Elvis back to us soon."

Surprisingly, during the filming of *King Creole* in New Orleans in early March 1958, Elvis expressed a rare change of heart suggesting that he *wanted* to serve (as opposed to just *willing* to serve). While on location in New Orleans, Presley couldn't escape being mobbed by fans. It was so bad that in order to exit his hotel, he had to climb up to the roof and then cross over to the roof of another building to get out safely.

"I had to hire a special security police to keep the girls off of his hotel floor," said *King Creole* producer Hal Wallis, "and still they seemed to manage to come in through the walls – in every direction."

Dolores Hart, who co-starred with Presley in both *Loving You* and *King Creole*, recalled how crazy it was filming in New Orleans: "All the time we [the cast] were having a ball, Elvis was cooped up in his hotel room, unable to even show his face on the street. I felt sorry for him, especially since he was due for a two-year Army hitch and I'm sure he would like to have had some fun those last few evenings. The crowds just made it impossible. Everywhere we went, if there was a slightest chance he would be appearing, crowds gathered and stood waiting even for a glimpse of the top of his head. Anything just so they could say they'd seen him."

At the time, when Elvis was asked by a reporter how he felt about going into the army, he said, "Frankly, it'll be a relief," suggesting that it would be a chance for him to escape the mania. Soon after, Elvis made another remark to columnist Vernon Scott: "My two years in the Army can't be no worse than the past two years. I've been on a merry-go-round ever since my records started sellin' real good - doing as many as 87 one-night stands a year, makin' four movies and cutting records."

The public backlash continued when word got out that Elvis was being granted a two-month deferment to finish filming *King Creole*. One army draft official resigned in protest. State Representative H. Nick Johnson, a 37-year-old Purple Heart World War II veteran, resigned his position in Harlan, Kentucky because Presley's deferment, which he viewed as special treatment, "made it impossible" for him [Johnson] to serve as a member of Local Board 35.

"How can I conscientiously tell other mountain boys that they must go when called, right while Presley is picking his own time?" Johnson stated.

However, delaying Presley's induction for 60 days from the original date of January 20, 1958 was a "semi-routine decision" for the Draft Board members to make: "He would have automatically gotten the extension if he hadn't been Elvis Presley the superstar," said the Draft Board Chairman.

But the writing was on the wall for both positive and negative reactions to Presley's upcoming service when two rival songs were released on the same record label in 1957 – the year before Elvis entered the army. "I'm Gonna Get Even with Elvis Presley's Sergeant" was a more aggressive song against the army by Janie Davids. As a battle cry of sorts for Presley's female fans, Davids sang: "With ten million chicks behind me, Gonna stage my own personal war."

However, quite disturbing was the anti-Elvis song called "I Just Want To Be Elvis Presley's Sergeant" by The Bobolinks. This song represented men who disliked the singer wishing to make Presley's life miserable. It seemed like an excuse for them to get out their frustration about this controversial rock and roll star as they sang: "I'd make him march until he fell / And wound up singin' 'Back-Break Hotel'."

Most radio stations refrained from playing these two records because of the controversy they created. Presley fans hated The Bobolinks song, while Presley-haters were upset when Janie Davids' song was played. However, according to *DIG* magazine, both records sold well via "under-the-table mail order."

The news about the new rock and roll soldier presented problems for army personnel. The Memphis Draft Board and Fort Chaffee army base started receiving an inundation of phone calls and letters from distraught fans once Elvis officially received his induction notice. One 18-year-old boy from Kalamazoo sent a letter offering to take Presley's place in the army, if they would let The King of Rock and Roll be released.

Milton Bowers said he received hundreds of calls about Presley. Some messages were threatening. A phone call from one woman said "she hoped my wife and all my children died," Bowers said.

According to Lamar Fike, who went with Elvis to Germany, Elvis in the army was bad for everyone: "The Army didn't want the problem of his celebrity," explained Fike. "Eisenhower put a cloak of secrecy around Elvis the whole time he was in. The president instructed the CIA and everybody else to leave him alone – 'Don't let anybody know what he's doing.'... It was bad enough to have Elvis Presley in the Army. He was more well-known than the president! They didn't want any problems."

On March 23, 1958, the night before he got inducted into the army, Elvis went to see the movie inspired by his own life, *Sing Boy Sing*, starring Tommy Sands. The drama, which was a movie adaptation of the play *The Singin' Idol*, featured the lead character named Virgil Walker as a country boy turned singing star from Louisiana who has a domineering manager named Joseph Sharkey. Virgil's religious background finds him constantly at odds with his manager, described as "greedy, hard-hearted and nasty" by one reviewer. Ironically, Presley's friend, Nick Adams, appeared in the movie playing the lead character's sidekick, an amalgamation of Presley's real-life entourage.

After watching the film at a drive-in with his girlfriend, Anita Wood, and friends, George Klein and Alan Fortas, Elvis and the gang go roller-skating. Elvis does not go to bed that night since just a few hours later at 7:00 am, he must report to the Memphis Draft Board. Meanwhile, earlier that evening, reporters came to Graceland and took photos of Elvis and his parents on his last night as a civilian.

One can only imagine how watching *Sing Boy Sing* added to Presley's sense of despair. Years later he recalled how he felt about entering the army: "Overnight it was all gone," Elvis said. "It was like a dream."

Meanwhile, the 1958 movie, *Sing Boy Sing*, was eerily prophetic with the main plotline of Virgil's grandfather, someone he was very close to, dying suddenly. Little did Elvis know that this plotline would play out in his real life just six months later with the sudden death of his beloved mother, Gladys.

2

HAIR HOOPLA

Although Elvis expressed outright panic to his friends and family that being in the army would ruin his career, he played the good sport in public.

"There's not much difference between this and making a movie," Elvis told reporters during his army induction. "In Hollywood, you have to get up at 5 a.m. and be on the set at 6. The only different thing here is that you don't have a limousine."

At 6:35 a.m. on Monday, March 24, 1958, dubbed "Black Monday" by Elvis fans, Presley reported to the draft board in downtown Memphis accompanied by girlfriend Anita Wood and his parents. They drove in Elvis' black Cadillac Limousine, while other friends followed in their own cars in what felt like a "funeral procession" as described by Anita. About 20 minutes later, Presley was then sent on a bus with 12 other recruits to the Examining and Induction Station at Kennedy Veterans Memorial Hospital in Memphis. His family and friends followed.

Before getting their army physicals, the new recruits were led into a reception room where a public relations officer gave them a short introduction on what to expect. That army officer was none other than the father of Presley's future girlfriend and fiancee, Ginger Alden. A photograph of Presley was taken that day with Sergeant Walter Alden who reportedly gave Elvis a dime so he could make a phone call.

While waiting around at the induction center, an autograph seeker approached Elvis holding his new greatest hits album, *Elvis' Golden Records*, which had just been released a few days earlier. When Elvis saw the record cover, he flipped: "Where'd you get that?" Elvis asked. "I haven't even seen it yet."

After getting his physical and being sworn into the army, which were both filmed, it was announced that Private Presley, assigned with serial number U.S. 53310761, was put in charge of the group to be taken to the Fort Chaffee army base in Fort Smith, Arkansas for further processing that night. As he left the induction station, Elvis said goodbye to his tearful mother, father and girlfriend. Other friends and family there to bid Elvis farewell were Lamar Fike, friend Judy Spreckels, cousin Patsy Presley and her mother, Clettes Presley. Colonel Parker would follow Elvis to Arkansas to oversee press coverage at Fort Chaffee.

Rex Mansfield from Dresden, Tennessee was one of the draftees to be inducted with Elvis and then boarded the bus to ride with Elvis to Fort Chaffee. He was amazed when he saw about 500 screaming girls waiting for Elvis at the hospital gates. As the bus pulled away, Mansfield saw girls running after the bus as long as they could to get one last glimpse of Elvis. Rex would become one of Presley's closest army buddies.

Elvis could not even escape the crowd of fans and press during the 4-1/2 hour bus ride from Memphis to Fort Smith. There was a caravan of cars following the bus, which prompted a police escort across the Memphis-Arkansas bridge. The bus stopped at a restaurant called Roy Fisher's Steak House in North Little Rock, Arkansas for dinner and Elvis had to be escorted in from the back door. Elvis and his fellow inductees ate in a private dining room.

That night, there were approximately 350 people waiting for Elvis as the bus carrying him and 21 other recruits pulled into the Fort Chaffee army base around 11 pm. Military police were on hand to control the crowd, and even escort Elvis around the base.

"I'm sorry I didn't get to see them tonight," Elvis remarked about the fans when he arrived at Fort Chaffee, "but I thought it was a little late for them to be out. It was kind of a surprise when they were here."

The next morning, there was already a pile of fan mail waiting for Presley at Fort Chaffee. The day before, Elvis had even received a telegram from the Governor of Tennessee. Governor Frank G. Clement, who happened to be a friend of Colonel Parker, praised Elvis for his respectful statements about entering the army: "You have shown that you are an American citizen first, a Tennessee volunteer, and a young man willing to serve his country when called upon to do so."

But The King of Rock and Roll was nervous just like any other guy his age - as nervous "as when I made my first stage appearance," Presley told reporters, "because I've never done anything like this before."

Looking back, it may seem like an insignificant event compared to everything else that would change when Elvis Presley went into the army, but to his fans, cutting off The King of Rock and Roll's hair was probably the worst thing that could happen.

One fan wrote to the public information officer at Fort Chaffee: "Please don't cut his hair. Can't you understand his hair is his trademark? How would you like for someone to cut off your trademark in a few minutes?"

And it wasn't only Presley's fans who were upset anticipating the army haircut: "I'm dreading the haircut I'll get tomorrow," Presley remarked on his induction day.

For the most part, Elvis did not dress rebellious in public. Most of the time he wore dress trousers and a blazer on stage. But still, it was Presley's visual look that played a large part in his appeal to teenagers. Most of the rebellion was reflected in his hair and sideburns. Take away those visual symbols and you would be taking away a source of The King of Rock and Roll's power - almost like the biblical story when the hair of Samson (of Samson and Delilah) was cut off.

This was not an exaggeration, according to some teenage girls who were so upset about Elvis' impending haircut that they wrote to President Eisenhower in 1958.

Dear President Eisenhower,

My girlfriends and I are writing all the way from Montana. We think it's bad enough to send Elvis Presley in the Army, but if you cut his sideburns off, we will just die! You don't know how we feel about him. I really don't see why you have to send him in the Army at all, but we beg you please, please, don't give him a G.I. haircut, OK, please, please don't! If you do, we will just about die!

(signed) Elvis Presley Lovers,
Linda Kelly, Sherry Bane, Mickie Mattson

Another fan letter, written to Captain John Mawn, public information officer at Fort Chaffee, got a bit more aggressive saying: "Elvis' hair might not seem very important to you, but it is to me and a couple million other girls I know. So help me George, if you cut off Elvis' hair, I'll walk clear down to Arkansas and not only will I cut off your hair, but I'll take your whole head off with it."

In the song about Elvis going into the army called "Bye Bye Elvis", the lyrics included "Don't let them cut off your curly hair." The song hit a chord with teenagers and, in April 1958, even hit the number two spot in the Ottawa Hit Parade.

Even though the actual haircut only took three minutes, Elvis sat in the barber's chair for almost two hours while approximately 55 members of the press took photos of him with his new haircut. The resulting buzz cut left only about a half-inch long of hair on the top of The King of Rock and Roll's head. Elvis was a good sport saying he had some "famous last words" about being in the barber's chair: "Boy, is this one a shorty," Elvis said as he felt the top of his head. "Oh, well, hair today, gone tomorrow."

Even Presley's new G.I. haircut made national news. Countless newspaper stories ran with headlines like "Presley Forgets to Pay for Sideburns' Clipping" and "Elvis loses locks but forgets to pay" noting that the barber had to call Elvis back to pay the "65 cents out of his own pocket for the destruction of his famous sideburns."

Notably, Elvis had already trimmed his sideburns for his role in the movie *King Creole* which he finished filming a few weeks before his army induction. Additionally, Elvis had got not one, but two pre-army haircuts during the week before his induction to lessen the blow. But even with his hair and sideburns shorter than usual, he still got a good chunk of hair cut off.

"It doesn't feel as much different than it did before," Elvis told reporters about his regulation G.I. haircut. "This is the shortest it's been in eight years."

The infamous haircut that occurred on Tuesday, March 25, 1958 became such a legend that everyone wanted to know who the barber was. His name was James B. Peterson and on that historic day, he had his brother-in-law Leon Merrill, also a Fort Chaffee employee, there to assist him. It was Merrill who swept away Presley's locks as they fell to the ground.

According to Merrill, the Military Police on duty guarded Presley's hair, not allowing even one single lock to be picked up as a souvenir. Colonel Parker commented the year before that he would not object if the army decided to sell Presley's locks to raise money: "If the government wants to sell souvenir strands for the Army Relief Fund, well, that's okay with me." If that had occurred, imagine the chaos that would have ensued over the years of people claiming to own Presley's hair. However, it is believed that Presley's hair that was cut off was actually burned by the army to avoid fans and journalists from fighting over it.

After the haircut, Elvis retired for the day from the press as he began his army life. He thanked the reporters "for the wonderful pictures and nice writeups you've given me."

The next day it was announced that Elvis would be assigned to the Second Armored Division at Fort Hood in Killeen, Texas for basic training and advanced tank instruction. This was General George Patton's famous "Hell on Wheels" division from World War II whose motto was "Victory or Death": "I don't want to die for my country," said Patton. "I want the other son of a bitch to die for his country."

In later years, Presley's friends would reveal that Elvis became obsessed with the 1970 biographical war movie, *Patton*, and memorized the dramatic speech at the beginning of the film.

Meanwhile, Fort Chaffee went down in the history books as the location of the legendary army haircut. Decades later, local residents of Fort Smith, Arkansas led a campaign to save the army barbershop and preserve it.

The Chaffee Barbershop Museum opened in 2008 and was restored to look the way it did in 1958 when Elvis got his G.I. haircut, with authentic barber chairs and grooming supplies from the 1950s. Elvis fans can see the actual room and re-live where Presley sat in the barber chair as a multitude of reporters and photographers watched him get a G.I. haircut just like any other soldier.

3

A FUNERAL FILLED WITH FANS

Private Presley was quickly adapting to army life in Fort Hood, Texas. He was going through eight weeks of basic training in Company A of the Second Medium Tank Regiment, 37th Armor of the Second Armored Division. Part of the training included sleeping in two-man pup tents and learning to live out in the field.

Elvis remarked that his favorite part of military service was basic training: "In basic, the Army force-feeds you in one concentrated eight-week lump most of the situations you're likely to meet as a soldier. You spend the rest of your time in service merely digesting this lump."

"We were taught how to fire the M1 Rifle along with other infantry weapons, and how to use the bayonet in hand-to-hand combat," explained Presley's army buddy, Rex Mansfield. "We were taught how to use the gas mask by going into a building filled with tear gas and being made to remove our mask... the confidence course, the 15-mile march with 70-pound full field packs on our backs, the week of bivouac... The training was very rough and tough and Elvis went through it all just like the rest of us."

Elvis had a brief adjustment period fitting in with his fellow recruits: "I caught a certain amount of teasing and bugging from some of the 'old soldiers' when I arrived," Presley acknowledged. "But that wore off. Then there was a period when most of the guys were sort of standoffish – as if I were a visiting celebrity or something. But that wore off, too."

Elvis was soon accepted among his peers once they saw how humble he was. As a result, he continued his charitable nature while he was in the army with his fellow soldiers. For example, at Fort Hood, Presley bought new furniture for his company's recreation hall on the post, and donated a record player. But Presley's generosity didn't stop there.

Elvis kept in touch with friend George Klein while he was in the army. He told Klein the story about how he was the only GI in his unit in Fort Hood that would wear a watch during training because the other guys were all afraid they would damage their own timepiece. However, they all kept asking Elvis what time it was which started to irritate Elvis. To make this annoyance go away, Elvis told his friend Lamar Fike to go buy several dozen watches for his fellow platoon mates. Lamar thought he was crazy. The next day when Elvis presented all the soldiers in his training unit with new watches, he told them: "Now don't ask me what time it is anymore!"

On Sunday afternoons, when Fort Hood was open to visitors, many friends and relatives of other soldiers would come to try to find Elvis and get an autograph. Women came "by the truckload" with as many as 800 curiosity seekers showing up. As one fellow recruit said, on the weekends Fort Hood is "flooded with girls."

Due to his previous JROTC experience in high school, Elvis was named one of the five Acting Squad Leaders in his platoon. Acting Squad Leader, which Rex Mansfield was also named, is equivalent to the rank of sergeant, although no one gets a rank in basic training. During basic training, Elvis earned medals for carbine shooting, tank gunnery and marksmanship with a .45 pistol.

"Elvis seemed to love every minute of it [army basic training]," recalled Rex Mansfield. "Maybe it was because he had been in that other world for a long time and this was a chance for him to just be one of the guys. And I think he loved every minute of it. He enjoyed it."

Since he started basic training, the army kept Elvis off-limits from newsmen and photographers. "We're all proud of him," said a Fort Hood spokesman after Presley had done five weeks of training. "He is an above average trainee."

While Elvis was busy proving himself in basic training, in the back of his mind, he was worried about his mother. Gladys Presley was his best friend. They had a very close relationship since Elvis was a young boy. This mother and son were extremely attached to each other.

The day Elvis received his induction notice, Gladys was devastated: "Oh my Lord, son, what are we going to do?" she cried. "I can't believe you have to go in the Army! No... no, this is not right. I don't want you to go! I'm so frightened! We will try to get you out."

As a result, Gladys was traumatized from the fact that her only son had to enter the army for two years. It caused her great mental distress on top of the fact that she had not been feeling physically well for the past year. Elvis was greatly aware of this fact. On the day he entered the army, he told a reporter, "I hate to leave my mother."

Elvis' girlfriend, Anita Wood, came to visit him for two weeks during the Spring of 1958 in Fort Hood. She was invited to stay with Presley's top boss, Master Sergeant William Norwood, and his wife Olley, who lived in government housing on the post. This was a special occasion where Anita got to spend time with Elvis when he was off-duty without the presence of his family or the guys. They had many private moments together when Elvis would open up to her.

"I'm going to marry you when I get back, Little," Elvis declared to Anita one night as they were relaxing in the backyard of the Norwood home. "I know it's been hard on you, not being able to tell the truth [to the press] about our relationship – and I appreciate your understanding. But you've proved your loyalty... You're the one for me."

Elvis and Anita also spent time on the weekends at the home of Eddie Fadal, who was a DJ that Elvis had befriended in 1956. Fadal gave Elvis an open invitation to come stay at his home in Waco, Texas to feel the comforts of home and even gave Elvis his own room in the house. Elvis enjoyed home-cooked meals by Fadal's wife, LaNelle, and spending time with their two young children, Janice and Dana.

Eddie Fadal described Elvis' phone calls to his mother from Fadal's house: "He put on a brave front, but he was very sad. He would get on the phone and call his mother... and for a solid hour, it was weeping and crying and talking little non-sensical baby talk that they had going between them, and mostly weeping. He was very sad about it all. He really thought his career was over."

Adding to his mother's distress was the fact that on May 28, 1958, Elvis found out that he would be sent to Germany in the Fall for 18 months. His mother and father were planning on coming with him.

To mark the end of basic training, Elvis received a two-week furlough starting on May 31. He drove back to Memphis with army buddies, Rex Mansfield and William "Nervous" Norvell. Presley made the most of his two weeks off. He took his parents, Anita, Grandma Minnie Mae and the guys to see his new film, *King Creole*; he bought a red Lincoln Mark III convertible, and he rented out the Rainbow Rollerdrome skating rink and the Memphis Fairgrounds to have fun with Anita and his friends.

Presley also squeezed in a recording session in Nashville at RCA's new Studio B. The session took place on the night of June 10, 1958 from 7 p.m. to 5 a.m. the next morning. Elvis showed up dressed in uniform. He recorded "I Need Your Love Tonight," "A Big Hunk O' Love," "Ain't That Loving You Baby," "(Now and Then There's) A Fool Such As I" and "I Got Stung."

Elvis loved to wear his army uniform out in public as he greeted fans at the Graceland gates. While on leave, he did a photo shoot with his new red Lincoln and one of the photos became the album cover photo for the *A Date With Elvis* LP. He also took a family photo at Graceland in uniform with his parents. The photo was very telling: Elvis looked relaxed, Vernon looked serious, and Gladys looked sad and pale.

As soon as Elvis returned to Fort Hood on June 14, he immediately made arrangements for his parents to come join him in Texas. He was beginning eight weeks of Advanced Basic Training in Tanks and was now allowed to live off base with dependents since he had completed basic training. The next weekend, Gladys, Vernon, Elvis' grandmother, Minnie Mae, and Lamar Fike moved into a three-bedroom mobile home near Fort Hood.

In early July, Elvis moved his family out of the trailer home and into a rented house in Killeen, Texas. During the next few weeks, Elvis noticed that the health problems that his mother had been experiencing had gotten much worse. On August 8, Elvis insisted that Gladys return to Memphis to be taken care of by her regular doctor, cardiologist Dr. Charles L. Clarke.

"I nearly went crazy when I put her on the train down in Texas," Elvis said a few days later. "She looked awful bad then."

However, by the time Gladys returned to Memphis, her condition was declining rapidly. The next day she was taken by ambulance from Graceland to Methodist Hospital. Her condition was described as grave, due to a problem with her liver.

On Tuesday, August 12, after a disheartening struggle with his superiors where he even threatened to go AWOL, Elvis was finally granted emergency leave so he could be by his mother's side at the hospital in Memphis.

When Elvis arrived at Methodist Hospital on Tuesday night, Gladys cried out: "Oh, my son, my son." Elvis spent all day on Wednesday, August 13 at the hospital with his mother. He left late that night as Vernon stayed by her side.

Early the next morning at 3:15 a.m. on August 14, Gladys Presley, the 46-year-old mother of Elvis, died from a heart attack due to hepatitis complications. Upon hearing the news, Elvis immediately returned to the hospital. He was inconsolable as he sank to his knees beside his mother's bed. He and his father could be heard "wailing" in grief down the hallway of the hospital.

That afternoon, Mrs. Presley's body was brought back to Graceland for a private viewing as hundreds of fans stood at the gates. A distraught Elvis and his father were seen crying as they sat on the front steps of Graceland. Tears streamed down Elvis' face as he told reporters that his mother's death broke his heart. "She's all we lived for," he sobbed. "She was always my best girl."

"I never saw a more loving relationship between a mother and son," Elvis' cousin, Patsy Presley explained. "Aunt Gladys was full of fun and energy. She brought out the best in Elvis. He inherited her vitality and humor. When Gladys was around, Elvis was never down or depressed… The bond between them was so close, no one could get in between."

Colonel Parker convinced Elvis that it would not be wise to have the funeral at Graceland due to security concerns. Parker made all the arrangements for the funeral to be held on Friday, August 15 at the National Funeral Home in Memphis. The funeral was made open to the public.

"Mama loved my fans," Elvis said. "I want them to have a last look at her."

A crowd of 700 people, including relatives and friends, but mostly female fans of Elvis, attended the funeral. However, since the chapel only seated 300, people had to stand in the hallways, while many more stood outside in the parking lot. Elvis had requested The Blackwood Brothers quartet to sing and they performed songs like "Rock of Ages" and "Precious Memories."

Elvis, Vernon and other family members "sat in a small room, closed off from the audience at the front of the chapel" which was surrounded by flowers. Elvis and Vernon were extremely emotional during the ceremony. Five policemen stood on guard during the service.

The large crowd then accompanied The Presley family to the gravesite at Forest Hill Cemetery. On the way, spectators lined the streets of the three-mile route as they watched the funeral procession pass by. About 80 Memphis police officers were required to handle the traffic and crowds.

Elvis collapsed at the gravesite of his mother saying: "Oh, God, everything I have is gone. Goodbye, darling, goodbye, goodbye..." He had to be helped back into the car after the burial was over. According to George Klein, Elvis cried for several days after his mother died and would walk around holding a piece of her clothing.

Letters of condolence poured in – not just from fans all over the world, but also celebrities. Elvis received telegrams of sympathy from Marlon Brando, Ricky Nelson, Dean Martin, Sammy Davis, Jr., Cecil B. DeMille and the governor of Tennessee. Also, a song was released by Red River Dave in tribute to Gladys Presley in 1958 called "(A Tribute to Elvis' Mother) New Angel Tonight."

It was true that Gladys loved the fans, and the fans loved her. A few weeks later, one fan in Texas shared with Elvis how nice his mother was to her when she made an impromptu visit to Graceland in 1957: "One day about a year ago I got a chance to catch her [Gladys'] eye when she came out on the porch at Graceland. She invited me to come in and see your beautiful home with all of its mirrors and the organ and the piano and the fabulous stairway and, well, everything. She was such a sweet lady. She said to me, 'This is all my son. What other boy would love his parents so much? I'll take you outside to see my pink Cadillac.'"

Elvis designed the tombstone for his mother, which included a Star of David to represent her partial Jewish heritage. That tombstone went into storage when Gladys' body was moved from Forest Hill Cemetery to the Graceland Meditation Garden in 1977. Finally, on the 60th anniversary of her death in 2018, the original tombstone was brought back out and placed near her grave, as Elvis originally intended. It read: "She was the sunshine of our home."

"She was the most wonderful mother anyone could ever have," Elvis told the press. "She was always so kind and good."

In a way, Presley being shipped to Germany in late September would help him deal with the loss of his mother. It was a beneficial distraction since Elvis did not have as much time to dwell on his grief because of the constant activity surrounding him in this foreign country.

But, of course, there were moments of sadness. As Sergeant Ira Jones described, Elvis would open up occasionally when he was driving his commanding officer around in his jeep a few months later in Germany.

"From about as far back as I can remember, Sarge, she was my whole life," Elvis said. "All the money in the world can't buy back for me what I want the most right now – my Mama."

4

THE OTHER GIRL HE LEFT BEHIND

While Anita Wood was Elvis Presley's "official" girlfriend as known to his family and friends, he constantly downplayed their relationship in public at Colonel Parker's request. Even though Elvis had been dating Anita since July 1957, eight months before he was inducted into the army, he was still having short-lived romances with other girls during that time. One girl who Elvis had been seeing almost as long as Anita remained a well-kept secret.

Singer, actress and model Kitty Dolan, described as "the least-publicized girl in Elvis' life", first met Elvis in Las Vegas in the Fall of 1957 when she was singing at the Tropicana hotel. She recalled how Elvis took her to see the Sammy Davis Jr. show at the Sands hotel in Las Vegas.

"It was too much!" said Kitty. "Sammy Davis does a take-off of Elvis at the end of his show, and Elvis loves it. He has a wonderful sense of humor."

Kitty later visited Elvis on the set of *King Creole* in early 1958 as evident in photographs taken of her with Elvis on the studio lot. She helped him rehearse his lines. She was linked with Elvis in the gossip columns several times and on March 11, 1958, Kitty was photographed as Presley's date at the Moulin Rouge club in Hollywood.

On his last Valentine's Day before entering the army, Elvis spent the romantic evening not with Anita (who could not be in Hollywood that day), but with Kitty. Elvis invited Kitty for dinner with him at the Beverly Wilshire hotel where he stayed during filming.

After dinner in the penthouse dining room, Elvis presented Kitty with a box of Louis Sherry chocolates. "We sat on the floor eating candy and watching television," Kitty described. "And I'd say, 'Elvis, try this piece.' He'd bite into it and throw it back with, 'I don't like this, try this one.' We were throwing pieces of candy back and forth, and I guess we looked loco but we were having such fun."

While the relationship with Kitty was not serious, she was still involved with Elvis through September 1958 when he spent his last days at Fort Hood in Texas. Dolan was quoted regarding her visit with Presley by gossip columnist Louella Parsons on September 23, 1958.

"It was a sort of farewell to Elvis before he left for duty in Germany," Kitty said. "No, we are not engaged – but I admit I expect to see Elvis soon again when I make a tour of Europe."

In an article in March 1959 in *TV and Movie Screen* magazine, Kitty shared her story of visiting Elvis at his rented home in Killeen, Texas the last few days before he was shipped to Germany. Kitty flew in from Hollywood and was driven to Presley's house by his father, Vernon. When she walked into the house, she found a living room full of girls. They were crying and fighting back tears as they were leaving since they had just said their final goodbyes to Elvis.

"If anything happens to Elvis," one girl told Kitty, "heaven help the army!"

There were a multitude of devoted female fans at the house ranging in age from 14 to 20. Some had traveled far distances from around the country to be near Elvis for his mother's funeral in August 1958 and then followed him to Texas for the last few weeks before he left for the army. Elvis was so touched, he paid for their motel bills.

"All of your fan club presidents flew down here, Elvis," said one member of Presley's New York fan club. "We didn't try to see you because we knew how badly you felt. We stayed around just in case any of us were needed."

During her three-day visit, Kitty and Elvis went to the movies at night or stayed at home. She said Elvis had a player piano, two electric guitars and an organ in the house. One night, Elvis had a jam session at the house and invited a group of fans to come over and join them to hear him sing.

Surprisingly, the March 1959 article written by Kitty titled "I Shared Elvis' Love" downplayed the fact that Kitty had a romantic relationship with Elvis. The content of the article was more about what Kitty observed regarding Presley's relationship with his fans.

However, around the same time, 21-year-old Dolan did another more revealing interview for a special magazine publication called *Elvis In The*

Army. The article was called "The Love Story He Hides... as revealed to the editor by his best girl." With Elvis in Germany in 1959, it was easier to discuss the fact that he had been dating other girls besides Anita.

"We dated all the time, in Vegas, in Hollywood, then at Killeen," Dolan revealed. "I've known him for over a year now but you never heard of it... Because I didn't want him to think I was using his name... But now that he's overseas I think we should talk about him. Everyone should. I want to keep his name alive."

Dolan, who was currently appearing at the Moulin Rouge in Hollywood, continued: "I feel perfectly free now to talk about Elvis. I was at Paramount yesterday talking to producer Hal Wallis and he says anything nice printed about Elvis is appreciated by the studio."

During her visit to Killeen, Kitty stayed in the master bedroom that had been used by Elvis' mother and father. After Gladys' death, Vernon had been staying with Elvis in his room.

One night during her stay, Kitty recalled: "At 2 a.m. we said goodnight. When he kissed me, I said with a little laugh, 'What is this with you and Anita Wood? I've been reading all the stories.' Elvis smiled and said, 'She has a good press agent.' And then he kissed me again, and I forgot about any other girl."

However, on the last day of her visit, Kitty found out that Elvis had made arrangements for Anita Wood to come join him just as Kitty was leaving. Not liking to be alone, Elvis often sent one girlfriend home as another girlfriend was on her way - a practice he was known to do often.

"El was so broken up after Gladys' death," Kitty explained. "That's the reason he opened the door down in Killeen. The kids that hang around are his escape. He hates to be alone."

As a fan of Elvis during her high school years, Kitty said she was pleasantly surprised of how Elvis behaved: "I imagined he was very conceited - which he isn't," Kitty said. "His face shows so much soul and feeling. His eyes are so penetrating, they have the most beautiful feeling I've ever seen."

Kitty said she had planned to visit Elvis in Europe later that year while he was serving in Germany. She was supposed to perform in Madrid and then would try to meet up with Elvis in Paris. However, it seems that those plans never came to fruition.

It is unclear if Kitty ever went to Paris that year and there is no evidence of Elvis seeing her while he was stationed in Germany. Kitty ended up getting married in 1963 and left show business. Although Kitty became another girlfriend of Presley's for the history books, she did have some great insights from the time she spent with him.

"Whenever Elvis talked about marriage he'd laugh or kid," described Dolan. "He just won't commit himself. One of his buddies said, 'You'll be 50 before you marry!'"

When asked if she wanted to marry Elvis, Kitty replied: "If he asked me to marry him I wouldn't, couldn't… You can love someone, adore him, but not marry him… I don't want to wed anyone in the business… I need a man who's very strong, devoted to me only, not to his career, too. When a man is all wrapped up in his career, a woman doesn't receive love."

5

GIRLS, GIRLS, GIRLS ALL THE WAY TO GERMANY

To steal the title from a future Presley movie, Elvis Presley's journey from the U.S. to Germany in September 1958 can be summed up by the phrase "Girls, Girls, Girls." Everywhere Elvis went in his long travel itinerary to get from Fort Hood to Friedberg, he was being chased by female fans.

At his press conference at the Brooklyn Army Terminal in New York before he left the U.S., Elvis was asked by one reporter: "Elvis, what's your idea of the ideal girl?"

Presley, who was getting very adept at handling the press, instantly replied, "Female, Sir!" which caused an eruption of laughter from the many newsmen and photographers in the room.

But it could not be a truer statement. Elvis loved all types of women no matter what country they were from, and he would prove to be very open-minded in his dating life in Germany. While he may have worried how his career would fare while he was serving his remaining 18 months in the army, he did not have to worry how the women overseas would treat him. The overwhelming welcome he received in Germany would be a telling preview of how European society would react to The King of Rock and Roll living on their shores.

Before he could board the ship to Germany, Elvis had to take one of the four special army troop trains with a total of 1,360 other soldiers traveling from Texas to New York. On the evening of September 19, Presley boarded the train at Fort Hood which then departed at 8:20 p.m. There were about 75 to 100 female fans there crying as they stood in the rain to bid him farewell, including several fan club presidents. Presley's girlfriend, Anita Wood, and father Vernon were also there to see him off.

Anita refused to be photographed because she said her "eyes were red from crying."

On September 20, 1958, when Presley's train stopped for refueling in Memphis, several friends were waiting at the station to meet him. One fellow soldier sitting near him on the train was surprised to see how Elvis reacted: "We had a long layover in Memphis... and I'll never forget it," said John Gilgun, who served with Presley at Fort Hood and in Germany. Elvis had "a steady stream of tears that went down his cheeks," Gilgun recalled. "It was really sad and quite moving."

But Elvis soon found something – or someone – to cheer him up. As Elvis leaned out the window to say hello to his friends including Alan Fortas and George Klein, his eyes were drawn to an attractive fan standing in the crowd. Her name was Jane Wilbanks.

"I had on this white leather coat and I had coal black eyes," Wilbanks described years later. "I kind of stood out."

Klein said that Wilbanks approached him and asked to be introduced to Elvis. However, Jane claimed years later that it was Elvis who had requested to meet her. Either way, Klein obliged and introduced Elvis to this "typical Ole Miss beautiful girl" from Mississippi who Elvis would call "Janie."

There was a photo taken of Elvis kissing Janie as he leaned out of the train window and she stood on her tiptoes. The photo got some recognition in the media, but it was quickly overshadowed by another photo of Elvis kissing a girl just two days later on September 22 as he was on the ship at the Brooklyn port leaving for Germany. The press labeled it as Presley's "farewell kiss" in America. The woman in that photo was fan Lillian Portnoy. However, it was Wilbanks, not Portnoy, who would see Elvis again in Germany.

With Elvis having been out of the limelight for the past six months, it was mayhem when Elvis left for Germany from the port of Brooklyn. After his farewell press conference at the Brooklyn Army Terminal, Elvis proceeded to walk up the gangplank of the U.S.S. *Randall* eight times so the press could get a good photo. Photographer Alfred Wertheimer, who had taken the legendary behind-the-scenes photos of Presley in 1956, was there at the embarkation. He said the sendoff was unlike any other in the history of the military.

"The Colonel had it all figured out, having the army band play 'Hound Dog,' 'Don't Be Cruel' and 'Tutti Frutti' instead of the usual military marches," explained Wertheimer. "That's the first time in history of the American Army that a troop ship left port where they didn't play John Philip Sousa marches. They played the songs of an entertainer! But, they still said Elvis would be treated no differently than any other soldier."

As the U.S.S. *Randall* embarked on its long journey across the Atlantic Ocean, Elvis could not even escape female admiration on the ship. Janet Day, a 13-year-old daughter of an Army officer, was on board with her family. She was one of many young children of military officers making the trek for their new assignment overseas. She made friends with other girls her age on board who were also fans of Elvis and they spent the 10 days on the ship in search of The King of Rock and Roll.

Janet and her friends were lucky to get up close and personal with Elvis when they ran into him in the ship's coffee shop. They asked Elvis for autographs and "he was polite about giving them to us," Janet recounted for a magazine article a few months later.

"He looked at everyone and said 'Hello,'" described Janet. "He looked down at me and said, 'Hello, Baby'… I was standing right next to him and he moved his foot. Onto my toe. I'll never polish that shoe again."

Janet along with many others were treated to the rare event of a variety show on Sunday night. They were not sure if Elvis would be participating, but they were happy when he appeared as the piano player.

"He sat down several times to play piano," Janet explained. "I guess he just can't hold still because he really was shakin' it up on the ivories. All the females on the boat - adults and teenagers together – just flipped every time he winked at them. Every little bit, he'd throw up his hands and wiggle which sent everybody into sighs."

The Captain said it was the best show they had in ages. The higher-ups had asked Elvis and Charlie Hodge to organize the show. Charlie and Elvis invited anyone with some kind of talent to participate. Elvis insisted that he would not sing, but he preferred to be a backup musician by playing piano for the performers. One of the guys had an accordion, and one day Elvis picked it up and started playing it for fun. At that very moment, a Navy photographer walked in and snapped a photo of Elvis holding the accordion with Charlie standing close by.

Charlie, who had also been serving in the army at Fort Hood, became close friends with Elvis during that voyage. Charlie, who had been part of a successful gospel quartet, would tell Elvis jokes and keep his spirits up as he was privately grieving the loss of his mother, Gladys. With Charlie playing piano, he and Elvis would often harmonize together on the gospel song "His Hand in Mine" throughout the voyage. "Charlie, you keep me from going crazy," Elvis told him.

On the morning of Wednesday, October 1, 1958, the U.S.S. *Randall* docked at the German port of Bremerhaven. Just like the scene 10 days earlier in Brooklyn from the American fans, an estimated 1,500 German fans as well as an abundance of newsmen and photographers were waiting for Elvis as he got off the ship. Elvis had to be escorted by military police.

"The Army is apparently torn between a desire to keep Elvis locked out of sight and a half-concealed wish that he had enlisted in the Navy or Air Force in the first place," wrote a columnist for an American military newspaper in Europe. "Everywhere Elvis has gone, the Army has been forced to make battle plans well in advance to keep the peace. Presley is far bigger than his company commander, bigger than the generals who watch over him, and the sooner the Army gives in to this truth, the sooner the furor will die down and everybody can get back to work."

Amid the frenzy of his arrival in Germany, Elvis made his way off the ship at Columbus Pier as he carried a duffel bag on his shoulder. He attempted to sign an autograph for an overzealous male fan who jumped onto the gangplank, but the military police dragged the teenager away. Presley then got on another troop train for a 200-mile trip north of Frankfurt to his base in Friedberg. One fan painted a graffiti-type greeting for Elvis in white script lettering on the outside of the train that read: "Wellcome [Welcome] in Germany Elvis Presley."

The next day, the army scheduled a press conference for Elvis at his new post at the Ray Barracks with about 150 members of the international press attending. He made a brief statement about his arrival in Germany the day before:

"I was very surprised at the reception," Elvis said. "I wasn't expecting anything quite that big. And I only regret that I didn't have more time to stay there with them. But maybe someday I can come back when my army tour is up, as an entertainer, and then I'll have more time and maybe I'll have an opportunity to make myself at home over here... *Arrivederci* – no, that's Italian!"

Presley's top sergeant, Edward Hackney, who was also at the press conference commented about Elvis: "He is under more pressure than the other soldiers because everyone looks at him, but I'm sure he'll do a fine job."

Asked about what he thought about German girls before arriving, Elvis said: "From all the pictures I've seen of the German girls, they're very beautiful. I think Brigitte Bardot is French, isn't she?"

6

PRESLEY'S OWN BRIGITTE BARDOT

Not only did Elvis Presley's official army duties make headlines around the world, but so did his love life. Upon his arrival in Germany, Elvis was linked with a 16-year-old German girl named Margit Buergin [referred to as "Margrit" in the American press]. She met Elvis during the first few days he arrived for army duty in Friedberg.

But they didn't meet by chance. Margit was brought to meet Elvis by Robert Lebeck, a German photographer for *Stern* magazine, who was on assignment to get some exclusive photos of Presley. On October 5, 1958, Elvis met Margit as he was coming out of the Ritters Park Hotel on his way to take a walk in a park in Bad Homburg. She asked him for his autograph and Elvis was immediately taken with her.

With the photographers shouting for Elvis to pose for pictures with Margit, Elvis grabbed her hand and led her to the park as they were followed by a large group of fans and reporters. It didn't hurt that Margit had a striking resemblance to Brigitte Bardot. Presley had made his interest known for the famous actress and sex symbol just before leaving the States for his trip to Germany.

At the Brooklyn press conference on September 22, 1958, Elvis was asked, "What would you like to do the most on your first leave in Europe?"

"I'd like to go to Paris," Elvis replied, "... and look up Brigitte Bardot." This response elicited laughter among the newsmen.

However, Brigitte Bardot quickly responded to Presley's remark via the press that she was not interested in meeting Elvis and criticized him saying he was not "refined." This prompted Elvis to reply: "Everybody quoted me as saying I wanted to date her. That isn't what I said. I only made the statement that I admire her and would like to meet her. There's a lot of people I admire and would like to meet."

Meanwhile, a group of photographers including Lebeck encouraged several photos of Elvis with Margit as they walked through the park. They asked Elvis to kiss her, so Elvis looked to Margit for permission. To satisfy the photographers, Elvis ended up kissing her on the cheek 16 times. These photos were soon published in Germany giving Margit instant fame.

But it turned out that this wasn't just for show. Elvis expressed interest in Margit and three weeks later, they started dating. Despite a language barrier, Elvis would see Margit several times a week. Elvis would go visit Buergin where she lived in Frankfurt, driving by himself, and sometimes spending the night. He told an American Armed Forces Network reporter: "I've seen her about four or five times already, which is more than any other girl around here."

"He is shy and rarely speaks about himself," Margit told a reporter in German. "We spend evenings listening to pop records or he would play the piano and we would sing folk songs. I was surprised he could play the piano so well. He plays the guitar and says as little as possible about his success as a singer."

One month later, the news of the romance along with photos of Elvis and Margit made it to the U.S. newspapers. Headlines included "Spreading Good Will in Germany, Elvis Dates Girl with Dictionary" and "Elvis Swaps 'Hound Dog' for 'Puppy'." One American magazine published the photos in a story entitled "Kissed by Elvis" in November 1958. In December, she was featured in a *LOOK* magazine article: "He's so different from what I thought he'd be," Margit was quoted as saying.

"The other night I said something about a puppy," Elvis told a reporter. "Well, she didn't know what the word meant, so she went tearing through that little book [her dictionary]. Man, it was funny."

According to the press, Elvis, who always gave nicknames to his friends and lovers, started calling Margit "Little Puppy." But Margit's mother said Presley's nickname for her daughter was "Honey."

During maneuvers in Grafenwoehr, Elvis wrote to his friend Alan Fortas in November 1958 mentioning Margit: "I have been dating this little German "Chuckaloid" by the name of Margit. She looks a lot like B.B. [Brigitte Bardot]. It's *Grind City*."

However, Elvis told his Memphis girlfriend, Anita Wood, a totally different story about Margit in a letter he wrote to her dated November 14, 1958: "The girl they speak of was a photographer's model and she was brought over by some newsman the first week I was here. I have seen her one time since then. She doesn't speak a word of English and I have not been dating her and I did not say all that stuff about seeing her four or five times and I have not tried to keep anything from you."

Turns out, Margit was getting almost as much publicity with the German press as Elvis. She became known as Presley's "fraulein," (the German word for young woman) and was the envy of female fans in Germany.

However, Margit's interest in getting press reached new heights in January 1959. Margit posed for pin-up photos which were printed in many publications including *Overseas Weekly*, an English-language magazine for American soldiers published in Frankfurt. In the article, she was described as Elvis Presley's "German girlfriend".

As a result, with all the interviews Margit did and now the pin-up photos, that may have been too much for Elvis. He preferred to keep his romances discreet - not only for the sake of his Memphis girlfriend, Anita, but also for his career. He reportedly stopped seeing Margit sometime in the spring of 1959.

As a result, Margit complained to the press about how Elvis dumped her. The April 1959 issue of the German teen magazine *BRAVO* featured Elvis on the cover with the headline "Scandal with Presley's girlfriend." However, a few weeks before, Elvis was labeled a "cad" in a March 16, 1959 article by the WNS (Women's News Service). He was reported as saying that he was only dating Margit for the publicity and that he "can't have any real romance" in his life at the moment.

"I feel mad and humiliated," Margit responded. "All the girls who envied me are now busy making catty remarks about Presley's ex-girlfriend. I'm the biggest joke in Germany."

Referring to Margit's pin-up pictures, Presley's friend and bodyguard in Germany, Red West, said that "Elvis was roaring mad. Elvis liked her a lot, but he can't afford to let a thing like that get out of hand. It seemed like Margit was taking too much for granted and after that, Elvis dropped her cold."

A German reporter, Thomas Beyl, who interviewed Presley that summer says Elvis got upset when Beyl mentioned Margit. Elvis left the room refusing to talk about her. Lamar gave Beyl the same explanation that Red West had stated, emphasizing that Margit had violated Elvis' privacy by doing interviews with the press about their relationship without his knowledge.

However, Margit was still seeing Elvis through the beginning of April 1959 - a few weeks after reports circulated that they had broken up - as noted by a reporter who interviewed Presley at his home and saw her there. Also, Margit was seen in photos with Elvis at a party for his platoon in early April 1959. So, it appears Elvis did not dump her immediately after the pin-up photos came out.

But no need to feel sorry for Elvis - the breakup did not leave him all alone. When he cut ties with Margit, he was already involved with several other women in Germany. Margit was just one of many girls that Elvis dated while he was in the service.

7

HOTEL SHENANIGANS

After arriving in Germany, Elvis got permission to live off base with his family under the military sponsorship act since his father and grandmother were his financial dependents. Elvis, Vernon and Minnie Mae, along with bodyguards, Red West and Lamar Fike, occupied four rooms at the Hilberts Park Hotel in Bad Nauheim (pronounced "But Now-hime").

"Mah (My) Daddy is here because mah Mummy died recently," Elvis told a British reporter, Ray Nunn, who took liberty in trying to recreate Presley's southern accent with the strange spelling. "He's lonely and Ah (I) wanted to cheer him up. And mah grandmammy too."

The truth was Elvis' mother and father were planning on coming with him to Germany before his mother passed away. When Gladys was sick, she pleaded with Minnie Mae to watch over her son in Germany.

"Germany was the best thing that had happened to her [Minnie Mae] in years," Elvis' friend and army buddy, Charlie Hodge, said. "Back at Graceland in Memphis she had servants that waited on her, hand and foot. She didn't feel needed. But here in Bad Nauheim she was needed again. She was running the kitchen and feeding a bunch of hungry people. They all depended on her."

During the month of October, Elvis was getting used to his new life in this foreign land. Upon his initial arrival in Germany, Elvis was assigned for the first few days as a jeep driver for Captain Russell, the commander of Company D of the First Medium Tank Battalion, 32nd armor of the Third Armored Division. Captain Russell had just recently been assigned to his position and was having a difficult time even before Elvis was added to the mix. On October 6, Presley was then reassigned to the battalion's

Headquarters Company as a jeep driver in a scout platoon for Sergeant Ira Jones.

"Captain Russell just couldn't handle the situation... Girls were trying to climb over the fence, go around the fence, under the fence to find out where Elvis Presley was," Lieutenant William Taylor explained. "Ira Jones was the best sergeant in the United States Army. Sgt. Jones didn't take any junk from anybody. If he wanted to keep the media away from Presley, he's the guy who could do it."

The newspapers had been reporting that Presley was initially assigned to join the crew of a medium Patton tank. However, before Elvis arrived in Germany, he said his last assignment had been driving a truck for four weeks in Fort Hood. The army announced the new assignment was made after reviewing Presley's military tests and records, and an interview with his company commander. This is the reason why on October 3 Elvis first posed with the Company D sign for publicity photos, but just a few days later was photographed with the Headquarters sign.

"The assignment of scout jeep driver is given to soldiers of above normal capability," an army official explained. "The soldier must be able to work on his own, map-read and draw sketches, know tactics and recognize the enemy and enemy weapons."

A rumor started circulating that Elvis was transferred due to a perforated eardrum which meant he had to avoid loud noises of artillery fire. "That rumor didn't make much sense to me," Lt. Taylor commented. "It's implausible that the army medical exam system had failed to detect such an ear problem long before Elvis was assigned to a tank company."

During the day, Elvis was driving jeep "HQ31" for the Master Sergeant of a scout platoon, Ira Jones from Arkansas, who had served in World War II and the Korean War and was a Purple Heart recipient. However, Presley was not just a jeep driver. According to Jones, each scout "was trained to operate in enemy territory with or without vehicles." The scout platoons were the first ones who would see the enemy in combat. As a result, Jones was quite impressed that Elvis did not try to get out of his assigned position to serve in the field with his Reconnaissance Platoon.

"As time passed, Elvis became our friend and we hoped that he would stay with us," recalled Sgt. Jones. "We could count on him to be a member of the team... By the time Elvis had been with us six or seven weeks, we were confident that he was going to succeed in the U.S. Army."

In contrast, Presley's living situation was not going quite as well as his day job. By the end of October 1958, things were not working out for Elvis at the Hilberts Park Hotel due to the presence of King Ibn Saud of Saudi Arabia. The King, who was there for his annual visit to get health treatments at the spa baths which Bad Nauheim was known for, seemed to attract just as much attention from reporters and photographers as Elvis did, and even more attention from the hotel staff. One of the richest men in the world, the sheik, who was accompanied by bodyguards and a harem of 30 women, would generously give out gold watches instead of signing autographs.

According to Rex Mansfield, Elvis "did not enjoy sharing the spotlight with the sheik." In addition, the sheik did not appreciate the antics of Elvis and his friends at the hotel. Mansfield believes that the sheik was the instigator behind the hotel management's decision to ask Presley and his family to leave. But Elvis didn't mind. Since he valued his privacy, Elvis was content to move to a more private hotel.

On October 27, 1958, the Presleys relocated to Hotel Grunewald in Bad Nauheim, about 20 minutes from the army base, where they would reside for the next three months. Between the five of them, the Presley clan occupied the four rooms on the entire top floor of this four-star hotel. Elvis lived in room number 10 at the Hotel Grunewald, which you can still make a reservation for in the present day. Fans used to leave their autograph books at the hotel desk for Elvis to sign – which he did.

In an interview with UK's *Melody Maker* in 1959, Elvis talked about army life: "I'm enjoying myself in the army. Living off base and having my Dad and friends around me helps a lot. And I'm not bothered too much here [Hotel Grunewald] as the elevator operators only bring people to my floor whom they recognize. Though I love meeting my fans… after a hard day at the base, I'm kinda beat when I get home."

During this time, Elvis became more interested in spiritual matters as he grieved for his mother. Elvis was reading books like *The Prophet* by Kahlil Gibran given to him in 1956 by former girlfriend, June Juanico. The book discusses various topics about different aspects of life bringing insight and greater understanding to the human experience.

While staying at Hotel Grunewald, Elvis formed a friendly bond with the owner of the hotel, Otto Schmidt, discussing topics like reincarnation with him. Schmidt even read the lifelines on Presley's palm. Schmidt also gave Elvis and his group special permission to smoke in their rooms, even though smoking was not permitted in the hotel.

"I can look you straight in the eyes without having the feeling that you want something from me!" Elvis told Schmidt, letting him know he was one of the few people Elvis felt he could trust in Germany.

At the hotel, Elvis was photographed in a V-neck sweater holding his new puppy named Cherry who was about 7 weeks old. The picture was featured on the cover of the German teen magazine *BRAVO* in early December 1958. While Presley was away on maneuvers, Mr. Schmidt helped take care of Cherry as he was suffering the loss of his own beloved Fox Terrier who had recently died. Elvis kept the male poodle until he moved out of the Hotel Grunewald in early February 1959. He gave the poodle to Schmidt, who then gave it to the hotel's housekeeper, Frau Reinhardt.

The night before Elvis was due to leave for maneuvers in Grafenwoehr, he threw a lively party at the hotel on November 2, 1958. He entertained his guests and friends by singing songs for them while playing his guitar. Not only did the music attract a crowd of fans on the streets below around the hotel, it also attracted reporters. A story made it into the American papers with the headline: "Elvis Set for Maneuvers After Giving Noisy Party."

It was reported that Presley's rumored German girlfriend, Margit Buergin, was not at the party. However, reporters asked Elvis about her and he acknowledged that he did like her. At one point during the party, Vernon Presley told his son to "play a little quieter." It was parties like these that would eventually get Elvis kicked out of the hotel.

A bunch of young teenage and 20-somethings attending Presley's parties did not fit in with the atmosphere of this conservative boutique hotel. The luxurious yet small 16-room Hotel Grunewald, with antique furnishings and crystal chandeliers, catered mostly to wealthy senior citizens who were visiting for spa treatments and a peaceful getaway.

Elvis, Red West and Lamar Fike, three young males in their early 20s, had energy to burn which led to shenanigans between them in the hotel causing daily complaints from the other visitors. Unfortunately, it was nothing new for Elvis and his friends to get into trouble with the management of luxury hotels, as they did during Presley's early days in Hollywood.

As Rex Mansfield described: "History repeated itself as the horseplay, ass-grabbing, pillow fights, wrestling and constant racket throughout the nights wound up irritating many other guests."

It was such an issue that even Colonel Parker heard about it all the way back in the States. In a letter Parker wrote to Elvis and Vernon at the end of December 1958, he urged them to maintain a low profile. Time would tell how long the Presley entourage would last at Hotel Grunewald.

8

ESCAPE TO GRAFENWOEHR

On November 3, 1958, Elvis Presley traveled with his scout platoon to the U.S. Army Training Area at Grafenwoehr (spelled Grafenwöhr in German and pronounced "Grafen-veer") in Bavaria for six weeks of reconnaissance maneuvers. This was the main training area in Germany for all U.S. troops and is located near the Czechoslovakian border.

While the battalion's tanks were sent from Friedberg to Grafenwoehr by train, the soldiers made the 110-mile journey by trucks and Jeeps in a road march. It seemed there were Elvis fans in every German town and Grafenwoehr was no different. The day after arriving at the army training post, Sgt. Jones encouraged Presley to take the Jeep for a drive in the nearby small village of Pressath to see if Elvis would be recognized.

And sure enough, "the place went nuts," recalled Jones. "People were pouring from all buildings on the street and shopkeepers were closing up their stores. Elvis, game as usual, dismounted and started signing autographs, while I begged the fans to form a line, a plea that was not heeded in the least."

However, within the confines of the Grafenwoehr training grounds, one would think that there would be no one from the outside to bother Elvis or his platoon since it was a restricted area. Instead, it was worse - there was a lot of bothering from the inside!

Elvis was off limits to the press while he was on duty at Grafenwoehr, which was and still is the largest American military training ground outside the U.S. Only U.S. Army photographers were permitted to take photos of Presley. But it was his fellow soldiers – and even his superiors – who wanted to get photos and autographs with The King of Rock and Roll.

"My security was going crazy challenging soldiers who wanted autographs," said First Sergeant Marvin Fuller. "There were even officers who tried to crash our lines to get to him. One high-ranking man tried to stand me at attention and overrule me when I told him he couldn't visit Presley on duty."

Even German soldiers wanted to meet Presley. The West Germans also used the facilities at Grafenwoehr and they served under American command at the training grounds. As evident by the many pictures of Elvis taken with German soldiers, Presley's presence definitely added to the spirit of partnership at Grafenwoehr between West Germany and the United States.

Elvis continued doing his best to serve as a regular soldier, which meant he had to "starve and freeze according to schedule" like everyone else. The conditions on the field were harsh in the bone-chilling German winter. As Lt. Bill Taylor described: Since "the tops were off all jeeps and the windshields had to be in the down position [for camouflage purposes]… moving jeeps created their own wind-chill factor. All of us who rode in open vehicles were just plain miserable. Many caught bad colds or contracted tonsillitis or pneumonia."

Lieutenant Taylor grew to have a friendship with Presley during the six months they served together in Germany. The lieutenant recalled a conversation he had with Elvis in Grafenwoehr where Elvis was tickled that Taylor's middle name was "Jesse" – the name of Presley's twin brother who died at birth. Elvis explained to Taylor that if Jesse had survived, he and his twin brother would have been best friends.

"Well, Lootenet [spelling to emphasize Presley's southern accent]," Elvis told Taylor, "it's funny about you and my brother both bein' Jesses. Good name – yeah, good name. I like it."

Elvis did not like training in the field in the cold and harsh weather conditions and voiced his dislike to Taylor in private ("Boy, do I hate this shit"). Another thing he was vocal about was the food. While they were on maneuvers, Elvis complained that there was not enough peanut butter included in the field rations. Sounds like he was missing his trademark peanut butter and banana sandwiches!

Another thing Presley was missing from home was his assortment of cars. While he was at Grafenwoehr, Elvis drove with Sgt. Jones and Pfc. Emmons to the Opel Wies car dealership in Weiden. The reason for the visit was allegedly a repair on his army jeep, but many suspected it was because Elvis was interested in seeing the Kapitän car made by the German car manufacturer Opel.

The owner of the car dealership, Anna Wies, had been notified in advance that Elvis was coming. After Presley arrived, all the staff gathered in the manager's office for a picture with Elvis and his two army companions. Word quickly got out in the small town that Elvis was there and people from the nearby stores crowded to see him at the entrance of the car dealership.

"He shook everybody's hand," recalled Roswitha Muller, a young girl who worked at the dealership. "We said we're not going to wash our hands for the next two weeks."

During this six-week training period at Grafenwoehr, the soldiers were allowed to return to Friedberg for two different weekends. The only catch was that it cost $6 for bus transportation, which many of the soldiers could not afford. When Elvis found out, he arranged to secretly pay for the bus fare for all of his fellow platoon soldiers who wanted to travel with the discreet help of Sgt. Jones. It was just one of the many kind gestures this "regular" soldier did for his fellow GIs.

Fellow army buddy, Rex Mansfield, spent a lot of off-duty time with Elvis in Grafenwoehr due to the fact that Presley's friends and bodyguards, Lamar Fike and Red West, were not around. Since they were not in the military, they were not allowed to come stay with Elvis since all troops were required to live on post during the training.

These training maneuvers were exhausting and required Elvis to stay up all night. It was here that Presley used amphetamines like Dexedrine or "speed" to cope with his overnight duty. At the time, there was not much research available about these pills or how addictive they could become.

"A sergeant gave Elvis and some other G.I.s pills to keep them energized," recalled Mansfield. "Elvis liked how these pills made him feel. Whatever Elvis' history with amphetamines was, he seemed well-versed concerning their effects."

Truth be told, by the time Elvis entered the army, he was already quite knowledgeable about all kinds of prescription medication. In fact, his mother, Gladys, started taking Dexedrine in 1957 to address hormonal issues and weight gain. When Anita Wood started dating Elvis in July

1957, she saw that Elvis owned the *Physician's Desk Reference*, which listed prescription drugs and their uses.

"He had marked up different pages that talked about certain drugs that he thought might help him in some way," Anita recalled. "Diet pills, vitamins, sleeping pills, wake up pills, sinus pills, and just about any other pill you can think of."

In September 1957, when Anita visited Elvis in Hollywood, she went on a trip with Elvis to the pharmacist where he put a large amount of pills in his secret safe that he kept in the trunk of his car. Most likely initiated as a remedy for his chronic insomnia, Presley had started his prescription drug use before entering the army.

In addition to the bookstore on the grounds at Grafenwoehr, Elvis was a frequent visitor to the movie theater on the base. One night at the movies, Elvis met a German-American fan named Elisabeth Stefaniak. Her mother was German and her stepfather was an American Army Sergeant. Elisabeth and her parents and younger sister lived in dependent housing on the post. She had been coming every night to the theater to try and meet Elvis, who was always accompanied by Rex Mansfield and another G.I. named Johnny Lang.

After about a week, Elisabeth got the opportunity to ask Johnny if he could get Presley's autograph for her. As a result, Elvis told Rex to go get Elisabeth and ask her to join him while watching the movie. It was a prelude of things to come as Rex Mansfield walked Elisabeth down the (movie) aisle. However, all of Elisabeth's focus at the time was on Elvis. She had been a huge fan of his since seeing him on *The Ed Sullivan Show*.

"I thought I was going to faint," recalled Elisabeth who was 19 years old at the time. "All I wanted was his autograph, and now I was invited to join him. Not even in my wildest dreams did I ever imagine this would happen. I was shaking from excitement and had butterflies in my stomach that wouldn't settle down."

Elvis and Elisabeth hit it off that night. He was very taken with her. For the next six nights, Elisabeth would meet Elvis at the theater and then he would walk her home. Elisabeth's German-speaking skills would come in handy insuring that her relationship with Elvis would not end once he left Grafenwoehr.

Elvis felt at home with Elisabeth and her family and would come over for breakfast while he was in Grafenwoehr. "He had a certain way he liked his food," Elisabeth explained, "and of course the army wasn't going to serve him anything different, so he'd come to the kitchen and he'd say to my mother, 'Ella, would you fix me some bacon, eggs and toast?' He had to have his bacon almost burned, and his eggs had to be flipped over 10 times. He'd come by in a Jeep, and I could hear the Jeep coming."

On November 27, Elvis dropped in unannounced for Thanksgiving dinner with Elisabeth and her family. This would be the first Thanksgiving Elvis spent without his mother. Elisabeth sensed that Elvis was missing his family: "I could see how much Elvis loved and adored his mother by the way he described how special she was and how much he missed her," Elisabeth explained. "He painfully mentioned that his dad was already dating other women, which brought tears to his eyes."

"When Elvis was in Germany [on maneuvers] he wrote a beautiful letter to me and my parents," recalled cousin Patsy Presley. "He said he had never been so homesick in his life. He wrote about the one Christmas when we were all together at Graceland, when Aunt Gladys was still alive, and how he cherished that memory… You couldn't read the letter without crying."

But Elvis also had something to celebrate on Thanksgiving Day. While he was in Grafenwoehr, Elvis was promoted to Private First Class (Rank E-3). This advancement in military rank symbolized Presley's transition from an apprentice or trainee to a skilled soldier. It also meant that Elvis could now wear a "stripe" (shaped like an upside-down V) on the sleeve of his uniform. The news was immediately reported in newspapers back in the States: "I'm proud to have a stripe," acknowledged Pfc. Presley.

"We hope nobody complains that Elvis was promoted before other soldiers in his unit, but he really tried hard to be a good soldier and he deserves it," declared the Army's Public Information Office (PIO).

At the end of November 1958 while Elvis was in Grafenwoehr, a *LIFE* magazine photographer named Loomis Dean got permission to come into the camp and take photos of Presley. The photographer got some great shots of Elvis after-hours informally singing for his fellow soldiers. A full-page photo of Elvis in uniform sitting down and playing the guitar was featured in the December 22, 1958 issue of *LIFE* magazine as part of an article titled "The Dictator At Home and King Away At War."

Part of the caption for Presley's photo read: "THE ABSENT KING of rock 'n' roll, Elvis Presley, sings to a sergeant in Germany where Elvis is a Jeep driver." However, the picture was not well-received internally by the U.S. Army's European public relations office. It was "hardly the image of barracks camaraderie that the Army sought to convey."

Captain John Mawn, public relations officer for the 3rd Armored Division, gave an explanation: The picture was taken "during off-duty hours. *Life* wanted pic showing him as former entertainer, now soldier. I suggested to unit PIO to attempt to discourage Presley from agreeing to guitar pic, but not to insist. Presley had no objection to such a pic... I do and intend to control on-duty activities. I cannot control off-duty activities."

Ironically, Elvis was not too keen on the photo either. As he told a girlfriend, he thought the picture was unflattering: "Do you think I look fat?" Presley asked her. "Are they trying to make me look fat or something?"

Before Elvis left Grafenwoehr, the U.S. Army scheduled a press conference for him at 10:00 a.m. on December 16, 1958. However, Elvis was nowhere to be found. After a rough six weeks of field training, it seemed that Elvis had been prematurely indulging in some R&R (rest and recuperation). He finally showed up behind-the-scenes looking disheveled with lipstick all over his face. According to Sgt. Jones, the soldiers in his platoon rushed to Presley's aide and helped clean him up so he would be presentable to all the reporters waiting. Elvis indicated later that the girl he had been kissing was Elisabeth Stefaniak.

At the press conference, Elvis answered several questions, including the rumor that he was spotted in town getting his Jeep washed at a gas station: "That can't be. I wash my Jeep myself." Ironically, while that may have been a true statement, after Elvis returned to Friedberg, Sgt. Jones arranged for them to have their Jeep steam-cleaned in secret before returning the Jeep to Ray Barracks. Turns out it was a common practice among the army Jeep drivers.

"We think he's a great guy," wrote a German reporter. "He greets us reporters with a smile and a wave of the hand, places himself in our midst and answers all of our questions. His appearance hardly differs to that of the other soldiers in the camp... Just two sparkling rings, which are probably worth about a thousand marks, give him away as the 'best paid U.S. soldier.'"

9

BLUE CHRISTMAS IN GERMANY

Elvis arrived back from Grafenwoehr the evening of December 16, 1958 which left about a week to prepare for Christmas. Back in Friedberg, Presley's platoon was working on their annual holiday collection of gifts for local orphans. Elvis reportedly made a visit to the orphanages in the area. Soldiers could donate anonymously to the cause, and everyone suspected that Elvis gave a sizeable donation because the total collected was much more than in years past.

The press inquired about what plans Elvis had for Christmas. In response, the Army released this statement from Elvis: "My grandma makes the menus and cooks the meals. I don't know what she has planned. I've been on a tour of training with my unit and haven't had time to do my shopping, but I intend, as always, to give presents to my employees, friends and different charities. As for gifts to me, my friends and relatives make their own choice of presents and I'm happy to receive whatever they choose."

At this point, Elvis could be content with himself as a soldier. He had proven himself to be extremely capable after enduring the harsh and rough treatment of maneuvers alongside his fellow G.I.s. "He knew the soldiers respected him as a full-fledged member and not as a wealthy star singer/actor," said Sgt. Ira Jones. "Now he felt he could talk freely with his platoon pals and not expect to see his words leaked to the press, to officers or sergeants."

Back in the States, Colonel Parker printed up 50,000 of his annual Christmas cards for the fans and business associates. The card featured a large picture of Elvis in uniform with a circular inset of the Colonel himself dressed up as Santa Claus. The card read "Holiday Greetings to You All from Elvis and the Colonel." A master at marketing, Parker had the card printed in "the Memphis and Nashville newspapers on Christmas Day, also in The Weekly and Daily *Variety*, *The Billboard*, *The Hollywood Reporter* and the *Musical Reporter*."

Also, Elvis would send out his own personal card from Graceland to his close friends and family. This card showed a photo of a winter snow scene at Graceland with several cars parked in front including a Ford Thunderbird and a Cadillac. Sgt. Jones recalled that he was very touched that Elvis personally gave one of the Graceland cards to him in Germany.

As the platoon was getting ready for their holiday leave, an impromptu sing-a-long happened in the barracks. Someone started strumming on an old guitar and Elvis was eventually asked to sing something. According to Sgt. Jones, when Presley started singing a rockin' version of "White Christmas," his fellow soldiers joined in and for a moment, their voices drowned out The King of Rock and Roll. But things quickly calmed down and Elvis was center stage. Per request, he also sang "Silent Night" and the room fell still. Presley's fellow G.I.s on their way out to start their holiday did not interrupt his performance, but would touch his shoulder as they each walked out the door.

On Christmas Eve, Elvis had a date with none other than Jane Wilbanks, the girl that Elvis was photographed kissing during his train stop in Memphis in September. The 18-year-old Mississippi girl was visiting relatives in Germany and Elvis started dating her. She had actually met Presley years before at the Mid-South Fair where she declined his offer to ride a roller coaster.

Elvis invited "Janie" to a Christmas party at an army captain's home, where she discovered that he did not drink alcohol. "I bet you never thought you'd be in Germany with Elvis Presley on Christmas Eve," she quoted him as saying.

She recalled the snow-covered German village to be a romantic setting where they rode around after the party. However, the romance of the evening turned to anguish when Presley cried talking about his mother Gladys and how much he missed her.

"Nobody else heard it – the great love and what she meant to him," Wilbanks continued. "And without her (at Christmas) it was so sad."

Elvis had explained the closeness he felt towards his mother a few months earlier: "Everyone loves their mother, but I was an only child and mother was always right with me all my life. And it wasn't only like losing a mother, it was like losing a friend, a companion, someone to talk to. I could wake her up any hour of the night and if I was worried or troubled by something, well she'd get up and try to help me."

Elvis spent Christmas day with his family at the Hotel Grunewald. His father, Vernon, gave him an Isana Gibson electric guitar which Elvis had actually picked out himself. This guitar is seen in many of the photos of Elvis singing off-duty at home while in Germany.

On December 26, 1958, Elvis attended the *Holiday on Ice* show in Frankfurt. Since the attendees were more of an older crowd, Elvis felt safe enough to sit in the audience, although he was still asked to sign a few autographs. After the show, Presley went backstage to meet the cast members and signed autographs for them. Most of the ice skaters were British or American, so Elvis enjoyed talking with them since they spoke English. He was even photographed helping one of them to lace up her skates.

"He did enjoy being able to talk to a girl and be understood without the help of a dictionary," reported *Movie Stars TV Close-Ups* magazine. "The girls, like girls everywhere, adored Elvis and let him know it. They especially wanted autographs… His acquaintance with these ice ballerinas had to be casual for they were leaving Frankfurt the next morning. Elvis could not pick out a Dotty [Harmony] or a Kitty [Dolan] or an Anita Wood to fill his empty heart and arms – even for a week."

Elvis enjoyed the *Holiday on Ice* show and the camaraderie with the dancers so much that he would go back to see the show again in Frankfurt on February 7, 1959. He went backstage and invited the entire cast to visit him at Graceland if they ever had a show in Memphis. After leaving the army, Elvis would attend two *Holiday on Ice* shows in March 1960 in Memphis at Ellis Auditorium. The day after the second show on March 14, 1960, he hosted a party for the cast members at Graceland.

Meanwhile, Presley's fan mail was overwhelming – in fact, it doubled when he went into the army. Once Elvis left the States, the base in Friedberg was receiving approximately 10,000 to 15,000 letters a week. The mail was coming not only from European fans, but also from Presley's American fans addressed with creative inscriptions like "General Presley," "Colonel Presley," or just "Elvis, US Army" with no address. Vernon, Lamar and Red would send the mail from American fans back to The Colonel at his office in Nashville so that he could take care of it. As for the German fan mail, The Colonel left that responsibility on Elvis.

Since about one-third of Presley's fan mail was written in German, it would be a big help to have someone who spoke the language to help respond to the letters. Enter Elisabeth Stefaniak. Starting at the beginning of 1959, Elvis arranged for her to move in to a room at the Hotel Grunewald where she would help Lamar and Red answer his fan mail – a full time job to say the least. Elisabeth learned, just like Red and Lamar, how to duplicate Elvis' signature for certain items.

"Foghorn," Presley nicknamed Elisabeth for her low voice, "the boys are going to show you how I like the mail to be answered."

When letters were sent back to fans, they were prepared as form letters on stationery with the words "From Elvis Aron Presley / U.S. Army, Friedberg Germany" printed at the top. An actual letter received from Elvis by a U.S. fan shows that the letter was printed on German paper stock. The fan's name was typed in separately from the rest of the black-ink typewritten letter and Presley's signature was stamped at the end of the letter in blue ink.

Part of the letter reads: "I'm trying very hard to be a regular soldier and do my job the best that I can, as all other soldiers have to do… But I do appreciate each and every one of you as friends, fans, and every letter that I receive, helps me so much to carry on."

But Elisabeth was not only there on official business. She also became Elvis' live-in girlfriend – although Elvis still brought other girls home. "Beautiful girls were constantly coming and going out of the hotel," Elisabeth recalled. "I had to painfully accept this, and just grin and bear it."

Back home, Presley's "official" girlfriend, Anita Wood, was waiting patiently for her Soldier Boy to return. In fact, she was planning to come visit Elvis in Germany, but Colonel Parker put a stop to it. Elvis said the Colonel did not think it was a good idea because the press would say they were engaged or married which would hurt Presley's public image with his young female fans.

Anita had been excitedly preparing for the trip by getting the necessary immunizations and getting the paperwork together for her passport. Needless to say, she was extremely disappointed on hearing the news that she should not make the trip.

"But he's my manager, Little, I have to do what he says about my career," Elvis told Anita, "and he says you coming here will ruin it."

The cancelled trip was what prompted Elvis to start writing letters to Anita to assure her that they had a future together and to counteract the news stories of Elvis dating other women in Germany, like Margit Buergin. Presley did his best to convey his strong feelings for Anita when he wrote to her in November 1958. Here's a short excerpt:

"Listen my Love never doubt my love for you, always trust me and believe me when I say that I love you.

It sure is going to be a blue Christmas this year. But in 15 short months it'll be over and as General MacArthur said, 'I shall return.' Have a Merry Christmas Darling and remember there is a lonely little boy 5,000 miles away that is counting the hours till he returns to your arms.

If you get a chance try to locate a record called "Soldier Boy" [by the Four Fellows]. Play it and think of me."

Anita later told Elvis that "Soldier Boy" captured "exactly how she felt about him." That was one of the first songs Elvis recorded when he came home from Germany in March 1960.

10

THE KING IS DEAD?

On Saturday, December 20, 1958, Elvis made a public appearance in Frankfurt to get the keys to a BMW 507 that he leased from a local dealership. Reports from December 19 stated that Elvis would be picking up the car the next day at the BMW dealership called Autohaus Wirth. The sports car was a demonstration model which had been driven by German racing driver, Hans Stuck. The car was rare with only about 250 built between 1955 and 1960, which is most likely why Presley would accept a used model.

Elvis was presented the keys in a "ceremony" by female German TV personality, Uschi Siebert, in front of several photographers and journalists. Hundreds of German Elvis fans crowded around the car dealership to get a glimpse of Elvis. The car dealership loved the free publicity they were getting by presenting the car to Presley.

Accompanying Elvis to the BMW dealership was his father, Vernon, his two bodyguards, Red West and Lamar Fike, and his current German chauffeur or "taxi driver" Oskar Mallmann. At this point, Presley and his crew had not been in Germany long enough to know their way around. On several occasions, they hired Mallmann to be their driver since he had a permit to drive American G.I.s and he spoke excellent English.

Oskar previously drove Presley to see Bill Haley in concert in Frankfurt in October 1958. Oskar described having to race Elvis away from the crowd after the show. He had to maneuver the car through the mass of fans who had discovered Elvis was there: "My biggest concern was getting out of there without having an accident," explained Mallmann.

Presley's newly-acquired white BMW 507 with leather seats, dubbed the "Presley-Wagen" by the German press, was a two-seater. Surprisingly, this cute little car would be the impetus for one of the "Elvis Is Dead" rumors that got started in German papers.

In mid-January 1959, a Frankfurt newspaper said it received "an unconfirmed report that Presley had a fatal accident with his sleek German sports car somewhere in Hesse." However, it is believed that a different BMW was actually involved in a fatal crash, but the press immediately assumed that it was Presley's car.

The story spread throughout Western Europe and all the way to the U.S. where it got distributed through a U.P.I. story. The rumor that Elvis had died was quickly refuted by the Army's public information office. As a result, headlines declared "Reports Elvis Presley Was Killed Are False."

When asked about this rumor in January 1959, Elvis replied: "These things happen. Once someone had me dying of throat cancer. I guess it's part of the game."

However, Elvis death rumors sprung up again in the Spring of 1959 after Vernon had a serious car accident. By early 1959, Elvis did not need Oskar's local taxi services anymore since he could now find his way around the area. Presley drove himself around in his BMW and he got a black Mercedes for his father Vernon to drive. On March 26, Vernon was driving home from a shopping trip from Frankfurt with Elvis' secretary and girlfriend, Elisabeth, in the passenger seat.

When Vernon attempted to pass another car on the Frankfurt-Kessel autobahn, that car suddenly pulled out right in front of him to pass a truck. To avoid hitting the car, Vernon had to slam hard on the brakes. This caused the Mercedes to roll over several times landing in another lane of traffic. Vernon remained unscathed, but Elisabeth was injured and taken to the hospital.

"The Mercedes was a total loss and the inside of the car was a terrible mess," described Elisabeth. "Broken eggs, Coke bottles, glass containers, and punctured flour bags were scattered throughout the inside of our car, on our clothes and in our hair. My head was cut in several places from the broken glass."

When word got out of this accident involving a Presley, reports spread yet again that Elvis was in the car and had died, sparking another false death rumor. This prompted an army spokesperson to release a statement to assure the press and the fans that Elvis was alive and not involved in the accident. The rumor was so prevalent in the U.S. that Colonel Parker's right-hand man, Tom Diskin, had his "hands full" in the following days and weeks trying to calm the American press and fans.

What the press and public did not know was that three weeks earlier, Elvis Presley barely escaped what could have been a deadly car accident. In fact, this terrifying incident could eerily have echoed a similar outcome as the one that took Princess Diana's life in 1997.

In an instant, a leisurely drive home in early March 1959 became a heart-stopping near miss. Apparently, one day when Vernon was driving the new Mercedes with Elvis in the passenger seat and Red West in the back, they realized that they were being pursued by paparazzi. Vernon tried to race away from a photographer who was chasing them in another car.

In the heat of the moment, Vernon drove through a railroad crossing just as the gates were coming down. The elder Presley made it through the first gate, but the Mercedes got stuck between the far gate and the train tracks. According to Rex Mansfield, in order to avoid collision, the Mercedes had to be moved sideways so that they would not get hit by the oncoming train. In the nick of time, Vernon maneuvered the car so that he, Elvis and Red were sitting within inches of the railroad tracks as the train passed. Once the gate was lifted, they were able to speed away from the photographer.

Imagine 40 years prior to Princess Diana's death, Elvis Presley could have been the first celebrity victim of aggressive paparazzi. This incident was not reported in the papers, although photos (shown in the documentary *The Definitive Elvis*) were taken by a reporter that day showing the Mercedes sitting in-between the train tracks and the security gates. Although the pictures reveal that there was a good amount of room for the car to maneuver, it was still a close call for Elvis.

Meanwhile, back in Bad Nauheim, Elvis loved to drive his white BMW sports car. His fans loved the car too and would frequently sneak over to where it was parked and pose for a photo with it. Elvis sent a picture of himself sitting in the car to his girlfriend, Anita Wood, back home in Memphis. During the summer of 1959, Elvis had the car painted red due to the problem of female fans constantly writing messages to him on the car.

There had been conflicting reports as to whether Elvis had leased or actually purchased the BMW sports car which could travel up to 150 miles per hour. Elvis confirmed in an interview that he had only leased the car and had returned it to the dealer in the fall of 1959, a few months before he left Germany.

In late 1959, there were reports that the BMW dealer in Frankfurt was offering "Elvis Presley's car" for sale. Surprisingly, when Elvis left the army and returned to the States in 1960, the car was also brought to the U.S. However, it is not clear why it was shipped there or for whom. Subsequently, it ended up being sold to a few different American owners over the years.

Rumors arose that Elvis gave the car to Ursula Andress in 1963 after they filmed *Fun in Acapulco*. While it is true that Elvis did give her the same model car, it was not the actual car he had in Germany.

In 2014, the American owner of Presley's 507 donated the car to the BMW Museum in Munich and they restored it to its original condition in white. The famous Elvis BMW 507 will now forever be available for the public to see.

11

FIGHTING POLIO WITH A SPECIAL FRAULEIN

A few weeks after spending Christmas Eve with Elvis, Janie Wilbanks was invited to stay for an extended period of time at the Hotel Grunewald starting off with the celebration of Presley's 24th birthday on January 8, 1959. The mood was more jubilant compared to the sadness of the Christmas holiday without Elvis' mother, Gladys.

"They had a cake and he sang and played the piano," Wilbanks recalled. "He played the piano much better than he did the guitar. I think he sang 'Happy Birthday Baby.' I gave him a royal blue velvet robe for his birthday."

After the party ended, Janie said Elvis took her to a late-night movie. He enjoyed her company because they had a special bond: "It was very easy for Elvis to relate to me because I was from Mississippi," Wilbanks said. "I was born in New Albany. He was born just 30 miles away in Tupelo. He could talk to me about eating turnip greens and how his family was so poor."

Back at the hotel, it was a slightly awkward situation for Elisabeth. Elvis informed her that Janie would be sharing Elisabeth's office/bedroom for those few weeks while she visited. Elisabeth was surprised that she actually got along well with her "competition."

"As far as Janie was concerned, I was Elvis' secretary," Elisabeth explained. "I never confided to her my true feelings for Elvis, nor the exact nature of my relationship with him... I think Janie and I realized we were just two of many girls vying for Elvis' attention, and accepting that fact of life brought us much closer. Janie was the first of many more to come."

Back in the States, Presley's birthday was celebrated with a special tribute on *American Bandstand*. The host of the TV show, Dick Clark, announced that he had talked to Colonel Parker who agreed to the special program. The show came about after a 15-year-old Elvis fan, Linda Deutsch, who ran an Elvis fan club based in the Jersey Shore area, got a petition of 3,500 signatures to make the January 8, 1959 show a tribute to Elvis. Nothing but Elvis songs were played during the two-hour show.

Meanwhile in Germany, Elvis had been busy giving back to the community. In mid-January, Presley along with 200 other soldiers donated blood to the German Red Cross at Ray Barracks where he was stationed in Friedberg. After giving blood, Elvis signed autographs for the nurses. Photos were taken of Elvis donating blood and were featured in several news outlets including *BRAVO*, which reported that many of their readers had written letters asking if they could purchase Presley's blood from the Red Cross "in order to inject it into their own veins."

Also in the giving spirit, a few days before Christmas, Presley took photos for the March of Dimes campaign with a young seven-year-old boy, Robert Marquette, who was confined to a wheelchair from the polio virus. Elvis went to the Frankfurt home of American serviceman, Master Sergeant John Marquette and his wife, stationed in Friedberg, to take photos with their son. These photos were featured in the National Foundation News of the March of Dimes in February 1959.

Anyone who dismissed these photos as purely a publicity stunt may not have realized Presley's extended history with the March of Dimes. In Presley's breakthrough year of 1956, he was photographed getting a polio vaccine in New York City on October 28. Elvis was administered the shot by the New York City Commissioner of Health and the Assistant Commissioner at a press conference right before Presley's second appearance on *The Ed Sullivan Show*.

Since an extensive list of Hollywood stars had a long history of supporting the March of Dimes campaign, it was not surprising that Elvis would take part in this crusade as well. However, it turned out The King of Rock and Roll was the perfect champion for this cause since, at the time, very few teenagers had gotten the vaccine, even though that age group was among those at the greatest risk of contracting polio, only second to young children.

Polio left thousands of children disabled, some needing years of expensive treatment and care. Sometimes the paralysis affected a person's lungs and they had to depend on an iron lung machine to help them breathe. Multiple vaccines were needed for lasting immunity.

According to health researchers, that single event of Elvis publicly getting inoculated played a significant role in increasing immunization levels among teenagers. Although official government data did not start tracking vaccination status until August 1957, an uncorroborated news report stated that U.S. vaccination rates skyrocketed from 0.6 percent to 80 percent in the six months following Presley's public inoculation. Along with the help of the "Teens Against Polio" initiative, Presley's participation had a great impact on healthcare in the U.S. As a result, huge amounts of money were saved on U.S. healthcare costs in the 20th century thanks to Elvis, not to mention the prevention of pain and suffering from this awful disease.

Elvis was photographed several times with polio victims before entering the army, including a special visit with the March of Dimes poster girl, 8-year-old Mary Kosloski, at his Graceland home in January 1958. Presley's efforts supporting the awareness of the fight against polio continued during his army service. He was photographed getting another polio vaccine while he was in Germany in April 1959.

But the first photo shoot in Germany of Elvis with polio victim Robert Marquette taken in late 1958 was not the last. To get additional exposure of these photos in movie magazines, another photo shoot was planned to get more glamorous pics of Elvis with the young polio victim. German actress Vera Tschechowa was hired to appear in a photo shoot with Elvis and Robert for *Confidential* magazine. She traveled from Munich to Frankfurt to appear in the pictures most likely during the last week of December 1958. The photos appeared in the January 1959 edition of the magazine.

The beautiful 18-year-old actress spoke English as well as German. Both her mother and grandmother were former film actresses. Vera was well-known in Germany and voted Germany's favorite pin-up girl that year. Elvis nicknamed her "Kitty Cat" for the shape of her eyes.

Although in later years, Vera would act like meeting Elvis Presley was no big deal, this was exactly the kind of opportunity she had been hoping for. At this point in her career, Vera had gained popularity in a handful of German films, but now she was getting ready for her theater debut in a small play in Munich starting on January 16, 1959. Most likely encouraged by her mother, who was also her agent, Vera came up with a great way to garner publicity for herself – by meeting Elvis Presley.

Vera actually went to Grafenwoehr in early December 1958 when Elvis was there and tried to meet him, as reported in the German newspaper, *Der Neue Tag*. She begged the army to let her present Elvis with a Christmas tree at Grafenwoehr, as documented by a news photo showing her standing in front of a sign at the training grounds. However, her plan did not go well and she was turned away by the military police.

Fortunately for Vera, her luck turned around in a few short weeks. Elvis was told that Vera was trying to meet him at Grafenwoehr. Presley's taxi driver, Oskar Mallmann, recalled Elvis asking him who Vera Tschechowa was. Mallmann replied, "She is a very well-known film star and she is pretty!"

The German magazine *Star Revue* claimed that Vera attended Presley's New Year's Eve party, which was soon after their first photo shoot. But one thing is clear: Vera was not in the initial photos that Elvis took with Marquette. As pointed out by author Andreas Roth, in the first set of photos Elvis took with the young boy, he did not have a stripe on his uniform. The day before, on December 20, when Elvis picked up his BMW, he commented that he still had not had time to sew on his new stripe which represented his promotion to Private First Class which he received in Grafenwoehr. However, the photos that Vera appear in show Elvis wearing his army uniform with a single stripe on his arm.

After their photo shoot with Marquette, Elvis and Vera posed for a formal portrait which appeared on the cover of the German magazine called *Funk Illustrierte*. With Elvis still in uniform, they were also photographed that day visiting the Frankfurt Zoo. Presley's driver Oskar Mallmann described the trip to the zoo as one of his "most beautiful memories" with Elvis.

In early January, Vera reportedly had a "date" with Elvis in Bad Nauheim. This would be her second visit with Elvis on his home turf. That day, she was photographed with Elvis by *Bild Zeitung* magazine at the Hotel Grunewald in Presley's room and then at the home of the Marquette family in Frankfurt. Apparently, they went to visit the young boy again and bring him a gift. Elvis is pictured in a block-style sweater with a ruffled dress shirt underneath and a thin dark tie.

One night Vera was seen waiting for Elvis at Ray Barracks, and there is a photo of them there driving in his white BMW sports car with Presley wearing his block-style sweater. Sgt. Ira Jones recounted that Elvis stopped by the barracks and introduced his date, a beautiful young actress, to the soldiers. Although the exact date is in question, Vera was most likely the unnamed girl that Sgt. Jones saw that night. Jones said the actress' visit really lifted the spirits of Presley's platoon buddies.

Meanwhile, according to Rex Mansfield, Vera invited Elvis and his friends to go see a screening of one of her movies at a local cinema. The group included Janie Wilbanks and Elisabeth Stefaniak, who translated the German-language movie for Elvis as they all watched it.

The German press would later play up Elvis and Vera's relationship as a full-blown romance and that he had moved on from Margit Buergin. Newspaper articles ran headlines like "Elvis fell in love with Vera" and "Elvis Quits Sales Girl for Starlet." According to Lamar Fike, Elvis was definitely interested in Vera, but Vera insisted that nothing romantic happened between her and Elvis. While Vera may have thought her visit in Bad Nauheim with Elvis was the last time she'd ever see him, he would surprise her a few months later.

12

THE END OF ROCK AND ROLL?

There was no question that the music industry was changing. In the late 1950s while Elvis was busy serving in Germany, rock and roll music in the United States seemed to be taking a backseat to the emergence of folk music and old-time ballads.

In 1958, The Kingston Trio's cover of an old Appalachian folk song "Tom Dooley" swept the nation becoming a number one hit on the Billboard charts and winning a GRAMMY. The song ushered in the folk music trend of the late 1950s and the early 1960s.

"It was just a huge, huge hit," explained historian Bill C. Malone, "and it set off a hunger, an enthusiasm for old songs – both real and newly made."

In the summer of 1958, Dean Martin released a cover of the Italian song, "Volare". When being shipped off to Germany in September 1958, Elvis was asked what he thought of the record: "I think it's great," Elvis replied. "I went out and bought the record when I first heard it."

He was then asked if he "might record something like that" – which, in hindsight, turned out to be a sign of things to come. Elvis replied: "Me record an Italian song? I don't know if I could cut the mustard (laughs)". Ironically, just two years later, Presley would record an English version of the old Italian song, "O Sole Mio."

In addition to changes in popular music tastes, several rock and roll singers were leaving the industry – some voluntarily, others involuntarily. For example, in 1958, Little Richard felt a religious calling and stopped performing rock and roll. He enrolled in college to study theology and started performing gospel music. Chuck Berry's career faltered when he was arrested in December 1959 for sexual relations with a minor. After two years of court battles which disrupted his career, he was sentenced to prison in February 1962 and served for 1.5 years.

In May 1958, just a year after his career peak with hits like "Great Balls of Fire" and "Whole Lotta Shakin' Goin' On," Jerry Lee Lewis, was mired in controversy when the press found out that he had married his 13-year-old cousin. As a result, his British tour was canceled after only three concerts and his popularity took a hit for the next few years. At the same time, Elvis Presley was out of commission for two years.

But what seemed to put an undeniable end to the era of 1950s-style rock and roll in the U.S. was the tragic death of Buddy Holly on February 3, 1959. The fatal plane crash not only killed 22-year-old Holly, who was at the height of his career, but also The Big Bopper and Ritchie Valens. This tragedy was so shocking and final with the loss of three young rock and roll singers that it would come to be known as "The Day the Music Died" from the 1971 song "American Pie."

On the morning of February 4, 1959, Elvis read about Buddy Holly's death in the *Stars and Stripes* newspaper while he was on duty in Germany and was saddened by the news. Elvis and Buddy Holly had performed one night on the same bill on February 13, 1955 in Lubbock, Texas. However, this was before Buddy was well known and he was at the bottom of the bill, so Elvis did not remember meeting him. Colonel Parker's assistant, Tom Diskin, sent condolences to the families on behalf of Elvis.

Meanwhile in Germany and the rest of Europe, rock and roll seemed very much alive. In fact, Elvis attended two Bill Haley concerts in Germany - one in Wiesbaden (October 23, 1958) and one in Mannheim (October 24, 1958). He was photographed backstage with Haley, but reportedly did not sit in the audience due to the hysteria he might incite.

The fans in Germany were out-of-control and caused a riot at a previous Haley concert earlier that month – so much so that it prompted Elvis to write a letter to *BRAVO* magazine. In the letter dated October 12, 1958, Presley urged the rock and roll fans not to continue with the rowdiness: "The originators of such troubles are boys who have to cause trouble everywhere. Don't let them influence you… If this trouble is going to continue, no promoter is going to book a show again."

The brilliance of Elvis Presley is that although the press identified him as "The King of Rock and Roll" starting in 1956, Elvis never defined himself by that. In 1956, he said: "I like rock and roll because it's selling.

But if I had my way I'd be singing ballads and love songs. Man, I'm no bopster or hipster. I'm from right back in the country."

Presley loved all types of music and he saw rock and roll as a trend that could possibly lose its popularity one day. As he stated in many interviews, he was prepared for that eventuality, and he would adapt to the circumstances no matter what happened in the music industry.

"I enjoy rock and roll," Elvis said in 1956. "As long as it lasts, as long as it sells, I'll continue doing it, as long as it's what the people want. And if they change, if it dies out, I'll try to do something else…"

Although Elvis still felt cut off from the music business while in Germany, it gave him a boost of confidence to see how enthusiastic his fans were in Europe. He told the press several times that he hoped he could come back and perform in Europe when the time was right.

Elvis was interviewed three times over the phone by *American Bandstand*'s Dick Clark while he was in Germany, proving that Elvis was still just as popular as ever in the States. Colonel Parker was working with RCA to keep Presley's name alive in the industry by releasing a steady stream of his music over those two years.

Meanwhile, with all his passion for music, Elvis needed a creative outlet while he was serving his time in the army. As witnessed by many friends and visitors, Elvis would often strum his guitar or play the piano and sing for his friends and family either at parties or informal gatherings. For example, while stationed at Fort Hood, Elvis was recorded singing at the home of Eddie Fadal in Waco, Texas at the birthday party for his girlfriend, Anita Wood.

In a letter dated January 9, 1959 to Elvis and Vernon, Colonel Parker urged Elvis to make his own recordings at home, specifically gospel recordings like "Just A Closer Walk with Thee." He suggested that it could just be Elvis singing while playing the piano or organ. The Colonel had the idea that this could be an Elvis unplugged-type of EP (extended-play) release with a possible title like *Elvis Alone* or *Elvis While Off Duty*: "I know that you could do a very good job on this and the kids would love it," Colonel Parker urged Presley, "as they have always been more interested in hearing you sing than the heavy part of music on records. As you know 'One Night' and 'Love Me Tender' sure did prove that they like your singing even without much music. Anyway I don't say that you will agree with this but it is something to think about…"

As a result, with a tape recorder that Vernon bought in Germany in November 1958, Elvis began making personal tapes of himself practicing during his downtime on nights and weekends. While in Germany, Elvis acquired a Hofner acoustic guitar, an Isana electric guitar, a bass guitar and rented a piano. The recordings were made over a span of several months ranging from December 1958 to April 1959. The exact dates are unknown but the bulk of the recordings are believed to be made at Hotel Grunewald between December 1958 and January 1959, and some at Presley's rented home in Bad Nauheim in April 1959.

As the Colonel emphasized, these tapes were to be made in secret. No one was to know about them – and no one did for several years. Six years after Presley's death in 1983, some of these rare recordings started being released to the public, with more to come in the years that followed. According to historians, Elvis made three tapes while in Germany, but initially only two had been found. Finally, in 2019, the full and complete set of recordings was released in a CD-set called *Elvis Made in Germany: The Complete Private Recordings*.

The recordings capture Presley singing all types of songs, in addition to he and his friends telling jokes and goofing around. Unfortunately, the audio quality of the recordings made on the tape player are not very good. There were a few songs that could have been released if they were recorded with better equipment, but overall, most of the tapes sounded like Elvis rehearsing rather than offering a final version of the songs.

Surprisingly, RCA had offered to supply Elvis with home recording equipment before Presley went into the army, but that offer was declined. In addition, Colonel Parker repeatedly turned down RCA's offer to have Elvis record in Germany or have him fly back to the U.S. for a recording session.

On the tapes, Elvis can be heard singing several songs that he would later officially record including "Such A Night," "Soldier Boy" and "Are You Lonesome Tonight?" As The Colonel requested, he also sang gospel songs like "Just A Closer Walk with Thee" and "His Hand in Mine." But even more intriguing are his recordings of lesser known songs like "I'm Beginning to Forget You" where he did multiple takes and one version is even sung by his father.

However, it seems that Elvis had no real intention to record songs on his own for future release as The Colonel had suggested. Most likely it was because Elvis preferred to record in a professional studio. But perhaps it was also because Presley did not agree with The Colonel's desire to bring Presley's voice to the forefront of recordings.

Especially in the 1960s, Elvis frequently got upset about how RCA kept tampering with his music. Even after Presley recorded the songs the way he wanted, RCA would go in and tinker with the sound. They often chose to make Presley's voice the focal point of the recording at the request of Colonel Parker.

The popularity of The Beatles in the mid-1960s would remind Elvis of what kind of sound he preferred on his own records: "He'd play a Beatles record and he'd say, 'This is what I'm looking for right here,'" explained Presley's cousin, Billy Smith. "'I want that drive back. And I don't want my voice to be brought out front. If it's there, I want the background singers brought out with me.'"

Meanwhile, Elvis was keeping up-to-date with the music being released in the U.S. while he was in the army. He had The Colonel and Presley's music publisher, Freddy Bienstock, sending him records, as well as his friend, Memphis DJ George Klein. Klein would compile DJ samples of the week's top 25 hit records to send to Elvis.

The Colonel was working as hard as ever to keep Presley's career afloat in the States. He had a plan with RCA to release new Presley records every few months. "One Night" released in October 1958 became Presley's biggest-selling single since "Jailhouse Rock".

"The new record is holding up just fine," Colonel Parker wrote to Elvis in December 1958. "Well over 1,250,000 [copies sold] to date and holding up very good. We feel it will go close or perhaps over 2 million in another month... Things are somehow looking up very well and we will keep working on all details from here to keep things rolling."

In addition, Paramount re-released two of Presley's films, *King Creole* and *Loving You*, during the Summer of 1959 to keep Presley visible in the movie industry. Colonel Parker played a role in marketing the films to small movie theaters.

The Colonel "was more of a promoter, not really a manager," Priscilla Presley expressed in a 2019 interview. "A manager really has to do what their artist wants, and Colonel had other ideas because he was about making the money for the artist."

A prime example about wanting to make money is when The Colonel demanded a $25,000 fee for Elvis to appear on Bob Hope's USO show in Germany. Bob Hope even went to the Army and officially asked for Elvis to appear, but his offer was turned down. The USO is a nonprofit charity that provides live entertainment for members of the military on location where they are stationed.

As The Colonel wrote to Elvis and Vernon in December 1958: "I see no point in having Elvis appear on that show except if he gets paid, as they show it on TV here for Buick and we all know they get paid for those shows."

1958 was a very successful year for Presley's career with all the new material Elvis had completed before entering the army. In addition, The Colonel was able to leverage Presley's absence from show business to get better deals with the movie studios. The Colonel would send Elvis and Vernon letters constantly updating them on the deals and plans he had in mind for Presley's career. They often included words of encouragement to boost Elvis' morale.

As he wrote in a letter to Elvis and Vernon dated November 18, 1958: "Have just received the report that 20th Century Fox also is picking up the new deal I worked on the past 8 months, so this brings the outlook for Elvis in a pretty solid picture for his future, better than it was before he went into the service... This also will prove to Elvis that he is not backsliding in any way. This now brings our picture setup in line with a very healthy setup for the future."

"They were an unbeatable team," explained author Peter Guralnick. "a partnership that no one on the outside could ever understand."

However, 1959 would require a lot more effort. That may have been the hardest year of work for Colonel Parker managing Elvis since his client was absent from the entertainment industry for the entire year. But The Colonel persisted and stayed loyal to his one and only client. With the help of his marketing and promotional efforts, The Colonel was able to keep Presley's name in the public consciousness for the entire two years Elvis was in the army.

"One of the luckiest things that ever happened to me," Elvis said, "is when Colonel Parker took me over."

13

A CASTLE FIT FOR A KING

At the Hotel Grunewald, Elvis and his friends were given repeated warnings by manager, Otto Schmidt, to stop their disruptive antics. For example, one day, Red and Lamar were wrestling on Elvis' bed and they broke it. The final straw came one night when Elvis and Red were having a shaving cream fight. Elvis locked himself in his room and Red lit a piece of paper on fire and slid it under the door to get Elvis to come out. The smoke alarmed the other hotel guests who thought the building was on fire.

As a result, Schmidt was forced to ask Elvis and his entourage to leave the hotel for good in January 1959. Elvis understood because he was well aware of the raucous behavior of his friends.

"I know that my bodyguards aren't angels but I do need them, and they have been with me since I went to school," Elvis explained to his army barber. "When I really think about it, they aren't just my protection against aggressive fans. I also don't like being alone, and their presence gives me a feeling of stability. I know they have their faults, but I like them."

Elvis did not harbor any resentful feelings towards the man who kicked him out of the hotel. After Elvis left Germany, he wrote Schmidt a heartfelt letter in August 1960 from the U.S. saying, "I am proud and honored that I was able to meet you and will always treasure your friendship. I hope that we will keep in touch."

Meanwhile, as Elvis began his search for a new place to live, rumors had already been circulating in the press for months that he was looking to buy and live in a German castle. "I can't imagine how that story got started in the States," Elvis said.

The truth is that it was not normal for an unmarried GI to live off-base. When the press found out that Elvis did not have to live at the barracks, the army public relations office was prompted to release a statement explaining the decision: "Private Presley is being permitted to live off post under the military sponsorship act. He does not qualify, by virtue of his rank and lack of service seniority, for military dependent housing. Therefore, he will be required to rent quarters on the Germany civilian economy."

One reporter ran with the story and suggested that with Elvis living off-base, only a castle similar in size to Graceland would be big enough to house his entourage, provide security, as well as fit secretaries to handle the high volume of fan mail he receives every week. Therefore, the only logical answer to Presley's housing problems would be for him to rent a German castle – at least that is what the local realtors were hoping. When asked about the prospect of Presley living in a castle, the army's statement included: "What he rents is a private matter as long as he pays his rent and observes local German rental laws."

By the beginning of February 1959, the Presley family had relocated not to a castle, but to a three-story house at Goethestrasse (Goethe Street) 14 in the town of Bad Nauheim. Bad Nauheim, located only a few miles from Ray Barracks, was and still is a world-famous resort known for its salt springs spa baths which treat heart and nerve diseases. In fact, President Franklin Roosevelt spared the Allied bombing of Bad Nauheim during World War II because he loved the town so much. FDR visited there several times as a child with his parents when his father sought a water cure there for his heart condition. (Note: Bad is pronounced "But" which means bath in German. This is why German spa and resort towns often have a "Bad" in their name).

While some local residents may not have been happy to have a young rebellious musician living in their neighborhood, they were in the minority. The local shops went all out selling Presley merchandise, and the town of Friedberg, which is right next to Bad Nauheim, recognized Elvis in their annual Friedberg Carnival Parade on February 11, 1959. The theme of the parade was "Die Wetterau steht Kopp mit Elvis und mit Hula-Hoop" which translates to "The Wetterau (local region) is topsy-turvy with Elvis and the Hula-Hoop."

Meanwhile, with the Presleys having a reputation of having been kicked out of two hotels, the landlady, Frau Maria Pieper, was able to charge them an unusually high rent at $800 per month – about 10 times what it was worth at the time. She also insisted on remaining in one of the rooms to serve as the housekeeper and oversee the new tenants in her six-bedroom house. Rumor had it that she took a liking to Vernon, and that was part of the reason she wanted to stay.

While not a castle by any means, the home was quite modest considering seven people would be living there. The home was fully furnished and had a full kitchen, a living room, a basement (used for storage), an enclosed porch, but only 1.5 baths. Elvis rented a piano which would become the centerpiece of his nightly gatherings and parties with friends in the living room. Frau Pieper's bedroom was downstairs right next to the living room, which caused her to complain frequently about the noise.

Surprisingly, one friend of Elvis was not impressed with the home. Heli Priemel, a 16-year-old German girl who started dating Elvis during the summer of 1959, described the living room as "inhospitable" having "dilapidated furniture probably from the '20s and '30s" and a "tattered sofa." The kitchen was "small and spartan," Heli continued. "All in all, this house didn't seem to me in any way a suitable domicile for a world star like Elvis."

A reporter who went to interview Elvis at the house in the Spring of 1959 noticed how often the phone rang. "Phone goes all the time," Elvis remarked. "It don't bother me when I sleep, 'cause I'm up on the third floor. But I think my daddy disconnects it after he goes to bed at night… Worse than in the States. But I'm used to it. It's been with me for four years now. There's an old saying that the time to worry is when they don't bother you."

But as equipped as the home at Goethestrasse 14 was, all the comforts of the United States could not be found in Germany. For instance, when Elvis moved into the house, there was no television. He immediately purchased one only to find out there was only one channel but it was German-speaking only. He ended up giving the TV to his landlady.

No longer able to run to Beale Street in Memphis when he needed a haircut, Elvis found a barber at Ray Barracks who he would return to about every eight days while he was in Germany. Karl-Heinz Stein recalled why

Elvis stayed a loyal customer to him over his 17 months in Germany starting with the first time Presley came in for a haircut on October 7, 1958: "The high tip, his words 'very good' and the bright laugh when reading his comic books made me come to the conclusion that Elvis felt very comfortable in my presence – without cheers and fuss... Even when I took over a [different] branch (the Mess Hall Barber Shop) in the same barracks, he soon switched to me."

At each visit, Elvis would pay Stein one dollar for the 35-cent haircut leaving him with a 65-cent tip. According to Stein, Elvis would always come at lunchtime because the barber shop was almost empty. Stein said that Elvis felt comfortable talking to him while sitting in the barber's chair "even if only for half an hour, [Elvis] found a little haven with me."

Stein recognized how special it was to have Elvis as his client, so he saved locks of Presley's hair along with the scissors, comb and razor he used on Elvis. According to Stein, Elvis was allowed to keep his hair one inch longer than other G.I.s.

"There was something different about Elvis, he was very special," recalled Stein. "He was so generous... so polite, so genteel. You couldn't say the same about all of his compatriots."

In Bad Nauheim, there was no space or security barrier between Presley's house and the street, so fans could come wait on the sidewalk and in front by the garden gate any time of day. Fans were ringing the doorbell constantly, so soon after they moved in, Elisabeth Stefaniak put up a sign announcing that Elvis would come out for autograph sessions every night from 7:30 p.m. to 8:00 p.m. to meet with the fans.

Reminiscent of fans congregating at the Graceland gates, the house in Bad Nauheim became a hotspot for Elvis fans from around Europe to come and wait for their chance to meet their idol. So many messages to Elvis were written in lipstick on the fence that he had to have the fence repainted three times in 12 months. As one fan joked: "If a teenager was considered missing anywhere in Europe, they looked for him there [at Elvis' Bad Nauheim home] and usually found him."

While many celebrities may have been annoyed by all the fans hanging around, Presley never expressed that sentiment. At Graceland, when asked if Elvis would call the police to make his fans leave, Elvis replied: "I'd never do that. These people have come from all over to see me. I wouldn't be in this house if not for them."

Because of Presley's generous nature, there are countless stories of fans meeting Elvis at his home in Germany. Some dedicated teenage fans would come wait every day at Goethestrasse 14 to try to get a glimpse of The King of Rock and Roll. They would watch with anticipation as Elvis drove up in his BMW sports car.

One fan would become a friendly acquaintance of Elvis as a result of her sitting in Presley's car with a friend and getting scolded by Vernon and Minnie Mae. Elvis also came out to reprimand her, but instead ended up inviting her and her friend to a party at the home of Presley's army buddy, Rex Harrison.

Her name was Siegrid Schutz. Siegrid was a 15-year-old English-speaking German fan who visited Bad Nauheim on several occasions. She first met Elvis and got his autograph on May 24, 1959 in front of his home. During the summer of 1959, she spent three weeks on vacation with her mother in Bad Nauheim. Every day during her stay, she went to Presley's home to try to see him.

After that first night when Elvis invited her and her friend to the party, she accompanied him often to places like the nearby field where he and his friends would play football. Siegrid took dozens of photos of Elvis by himself and Elvis signing autographs with her and other fans. She also took photos of Elvis on the football field and eating dinner with his fellow G.I.s.

"Elvis was loved by all of us because he was always polite, very friendly and took time for us fans," wrote Schutz many years later. "As you can see, he was in the truest sense of the word 'A star you can touch,' without being starry. It has remained an unforgettable time in my youth to this day, which I wouldn't want to miss, namely to meet Elvis up close."

But it was not just teenage girls who wanted to meet Presley. Reporter Thomas Beyl who went to interview Elvis at his home in Bad Nauheim in the summer of 1959 observed that the crowd of fans gathered at Goethestrasse 14 included "men, mature mothers with their young ones as well as curious elderly spa visitors who had heard about the 'King of Teens' and want to take a look at him."

Beyl witnessed Presley signing autographs one hot August night not just for the 30-minute promised time slot, but instead for three long hours. Then at 3 a.m., the Presley household was awakened when the police rang the doorbell to inform Elvis that five teens from Sweden had been arrested for climbing over the fence at the Bad Nauheim house. Instead of being angry, Elvis invited them in for a cup of coffee.

Presley's daily routine of being a soldier affected everyone in the house and the fans got to know his schedule by heart. Elvis got up at 5:30 a.m. and would eat breakfast prepared by his grandmother. Lamar, Red, and Elisabeth all had to get up too to keep Elvis company. Then after Elvis left at 6:50 a.m. to drive to Ray Barracks, which was only a six-minute drive, they would all go back to bed.

Elvis would return for his afternoon break usually between 11:45 a.m. and 12:45 p.m. so he could bypass the army's food and enjoy Minnie Mae's southern cooking for lunch as well. As Elvis drove up to the house, if there was a small crowd of only a dozen people, he would stop in front to sign autographs for 15 minutes before eating lunch. At other times, if there was a large crowd, he would have to sneak into the house from the back entrance. He would park on a side street and jump over bushes and fences to get to the back door.

One day he was leaving the house with just enough time to return to the barracks by 2:00 p.m. If he was late, he would be punished by his superiors. However, there were a group of deaf boys who were waiting to get autographs from Elvis. When he realized they were deaf, he spent an extra amount of time with them, all the while knowing that he was late to return to army duty. Luckily, reporter Thomas Beyl was on-hand to translate between Elvis and the boys by writing on paper to them in German.

Elvis was curious to know how they could listen to music since they were deaf. They explained to him that they had special amplifying equipment at their school in Friedberg. This prompted Elvis to want to visit their school. He drove the boys back to their school and signed autographs for their classmates. He then met the headmaster of the school who told Elvis about a charity raffle they were having. On the spot, Elvis decided to donate one of his army jackets so he could cut it up into pieces and sign each piece for the raffle.

As a result, Elvis did not make it back to the army base until 3:15 p.m. He had to serve K.P. duty that night (Kitchen Patrol) – "a special punishment for latecomers which means scrubbing the floors and peeling potatoes for a few hundred G.I.s." He did not make it back home until 8:00

p.m. (over two hours later than normal) just in time for the autograph session in front of his house.

One dedicated male fan who went to many of the autograph sessions was a 16-year-old high school student named Claus-Kurt Ilge. Ilge lived in Friedberg and would listen to Presley's music on the American radio station AFN (American Forces Network). In February 1959, Claus started going almost every day to Presley's Bad Nauheim home to try and see Elvis. He became part of a small group of committed fans who waited all hours of the day to see The King of Rock and Roll.

"We teenagers knew exactly when Elvis was coming off duty," recalled Ilge. "We were informed of almost the entire daily routine. We besieged the house day and night. We had a real 'club' – several people took turns keeping watch and keeping each other informed: 'Now he's gone' or 'He's coming back soon.'"

Ilge first met Elvis in October 1958 when Elvis arrived in Germany. He waited outside Ray Barracks to see Elvis. Claus had an advantage since he was a paperboy and always had the latest German newspaper in hand. Elvis wanted to buy one, but Claus gave it to him for free. Subsequently, Ilge would frequently bring Elvis the latest German newspapers when there was a story about him. Ilge soon became a familiar face to the megastar and Presley called him "The Boy from Friedberg."

One day, Ilge concocted a plan where he would ride his bike in the early morning to Presley's home. Then he was bold enough to ask Elvis, who was on his way to the barracks, to give him a ride back to Friedberg, and Elvis agreed! Claus got to ride with The King in his Mercedes on the short journey to Friedberg as Presley's song "One Night" played on the radio in the car.

"Elvis was an idol, but he was also a very polite, courteous young man," Ilge described. "I would have loved to have had a brother like that… He had no starry airs, gave everyone autographs, was there for his fans, had himself photographed with everyone. Just as the fans wanted it to be."

Claus says he only saw Presley get mad once. Elvis was meticulous about his army uniform and did not want anyone to touch it. One afternoon some kids grabbed his uniform hat off his head. Elvis got very mad and went in the house and did not come out later for his autograph session. By the time the weekly radio special called *It's Elvis Time* started playing at 9:00 p.m., there were only about five Elvis "club" members remaining.

Claus placed his transistor radio on the gate post for all to hear the 15-minute Wednesday evening show broadcast on Radio Luxembourg. This must have prompted Elvis to come back out, although he proclaimed: "No autographs, no photos." Instead, he listened to the show with the small group of fans as he sang along and clowned around.

By the time Elvis left Germany in March 1960, Claus says he obtained 304 authentic autographs from Elvis. He observed that if you left pictures at the house for Elvis to sign, someone else may have signed them (like Elisabeth, Red or Lamar), which resulted in countless fake autographs of Presley floating around. By watching Elvis autograph in person, Claus could tell which ones were real compared to the fakes.

In addition, Presley left Ilge with some more precious souvenirs. When Elvis was packing to leave Germany, he came out of the house and invited Claus inside. He told him he could have his record player and tape recorder. Ilge was so honored that instead of risking them falling off his bike, he carried them home on foot and still owns them to this day!

A friend of Claus' from the Elvis "club" was 14-year-old Angelika Springauf, who could truly call herself Elvis' neighbor. She lived only a three-minute walk away from Presley's Bad Nauheim home. But she first met Elvis at a local movie theater in Friedberg. In October 1958, she and a girlfriend found out that Elvis had gone to the movies at the local cinema where he was watching a matinee showing of *The Bravados* starring Gregory Peck. They waited outside the back door of the theater for Presley to leave.

Angelika and her friend, Ingrid, were surprised to see Elvis come out by himself. He happily signed autographs for the two girls, as he seemed very relaxed and friendly. As a result, the girls became devoted to seeing Elvis as much as they could.

"He's quite normal," Angelika recalled. "No different from the guys from the neighborhood."

Well, maybe a little different. A young 11-year-old German fan, Elvira, was lucky enough to see Elvis pull up one day in his BMW sports car with an unidentified blonde woman. Elvira got to experience Elvis up close smelling his cologne and noticing the sapphire ring on his pinky finger. She was not used to seeing men wear jewelry.

When Elvis moved to Goethestrasse 14, Angelika figured out the best time to wait for Elvis was when Red and Lamar went to the nearby Beck's bar, since Elvis would not go with them. Elvis would come out by himself and tease the girls and pull their ponytails, and for the guys, he would give generous tips for a good car wash.

One day, Angelika and her friend saw Elvis riding a bike in the neighborhood. They tried to walk beside him as he rode, but "he grinned and rode faster." They decided to go wait for him at his home instead. When he came back, he showed his new bike to them. He later gave the bike away to a boy in the neighborhood.

Once when Angelika said something cute in her broken English, Elvis "gently strokes her cheek with his hand. But that is the highest of the feelings," explained Angelika in 2015 (translated from German). "The King likes to be swarmed by the girls, but it remains harmless. The times were different than they are today. The affectionate cheek stroker is something special."

Sometimes, Angelika would bring her battery-operated record player to Presley's home. She would set it up on the gate post and the crowd would listen to records. When Elvis was there, he would happily look through the records and choose one to play, although never one of his own songs.

Of the many hours and days that Angelika spent waiting at Presley's home, she often witnessed Elvis' army buddies like Charlie Hodge and Rex Mansfield coming over at night to sing gospel songs. They could be seen gathered around the piano in the living room, and their singing could be heard by the fans outside. Elvis felt at home in Germany, Angelika was sure of that.

14

THE ROMANCE THAT NEVER WAS

Having been a dutiful soldier for his first five months in Germany, by early March 1959, Elvis was ready to spread his wings. He was granted a four-day leave to visit Munich, which was approximately 4-5 hours away by car. Presley's main reason for traveling to Munich was to visit actress Vera Tschechowa, the 18-year-old German actress, who he had spent time with personally and professionally two months earlier.

Historians had assumed that Elvis arrived in Munich on March 3. However, Presley's official "Request and Authority for Absence" form states that requested leave with the destination of Munich, Germany was granted to him from March 2-5, 1959, so he was actually there for four days, not three as previously believed.

On Monday, March 2, Elvis, accompanied by Lamar, Red and his chauffeur Joseph Wehrheim, showed up unannounced at the address of Fresenius Street 40 (Freseniusstrasse 40), the Munich home of Vera and her mother. What seemed to have started out as an innocent leisure trip for Private Presley turned into a publicity stunt for the young German actress.

When Elvis arrived, Vera was not home, so her mother, Ada, invited Presley and his friends in. She also invited a photographer from *Bild Zeitung*, a German gossip tabloid, inside to take photos. Having been an actress, Ada, who was now her daughter's talent agent, realized that the free publicity showing The King of Rock and Roll visiting her daughter would be priceless.

The word immediately spread in Vera's neighborhood that Elvis was staying at her house. This caused chaos as teenagers descended onto the Tschechowa house for days trying to get a glimpse of Elvis. One paper reported that as a result of Presley's visit, the Tschechowa's doorbell had been broken, their fence had been damaged from fans climbing on it, the police had to be called daily, and the neighbors complained about the noise from the fans that lasted until 4 a.m. every night.

There were photos taken inside the house of Ada attending to her famous guest by pouring milk for Elvis, and other photos of Elvis waiting around in the house. Elvis was wearing the same white-striped jacket that he wore on *The Milton Berle Show* in June 1956. In addition, Ada was shown fixing Presley's tie "because, naturally, he wanted to see Vera on stage," explained *BRAVO* magazine.

Vera was making her theater debut in a play at Theater Unter den Arkaden, called *Der Verfuhrer*, meaning "The Seducer." She had performed there every night for almost two months since January 16. Elvis was interested in seeing Vera's performance even though the dialogue was spoken in German and he would not understand it.

According to Vera, Elvis rented the entire theater of 143 seats for just he, Red and Lamar. Vera said she found this extremely awkward and embarrassing playing to an audience of only three. Meanwhile, Vera's mother tried to think of places Elvis could go without being bothered by fans. One local paper reported that the famous beer hall, Hofbrauhaus, urged Elvis not to visit until further notice.

"After all, he only has a few days of vacation and he doesn't like being wedged in by autograph hunters," Ada said.

After the play, reports said that Vera and her mother went to dinner with Elvis, Lamar and Red at the exclusive Zur Kanne restaurant. Ada had invited Elvis and his friends to stay over at their house.

On Tuesday March 3, Elvis and Vera drove her mother's sports car to the Bavaria Film studios at Geiselgasteig. Since Presley's Mercedes needed maintenance, Ada let Elvis drive her car. They went to visit the set of the American television series, *Tales of The Vikings*, starring actor Jerome Courtland, which was filming on-location in Germany. Vera appeared in one of the episodes which would air later that year on October 20, 1959.

As usual on this trip, Elvis and Vera were followed around by the press. One reporter noted how everyone who met Elvis at the film studio had a positive experience with him: "The most impressive thing about him [Elvis] is that he is not trying to impress at all," said the public relations manager of Bavaria studios.

Elvis and Vera were escorted around the studio for a tour and they had lunch at the canteen. In the afternoon, Elvis and Vera were pictured going on a boat ride at Lake Starnberg. Later that night, Elvis again attended Vera's play.

Surprisingly, Vera started receiving some negative feedback from her fans about her involvement with Elvis. She received letters from her many fan clubs expressing disproval of Presley saying he was "cheap… uncouth…a gangster."

Vera responded at the time in a positive light: "Elvis is very much misunderstood," she said. "He is a sensitive, honest and good-hearted friend."

Many photos were taken that night of Elvis signing autographs for fans outside the theater. He was wearing a dark jacket with a thick sweater underneath. He had not come to Munich fully prepared with the appropriate clothes, so the next day he sent his driver out to purchase some dress shirts for him. This provided a point of contention with Vera's many German fans: "Anyone who would attend theater without a shirt or necktie is no gentleman."

Vera's mother, a savvy talent agent catering to the German youth market, stuck up for Elvis: "Elvis is a simple, intelligent boy, who though he is rich, never forgets he once drove a truck for 35 dollars a week. He does his work as a soldier without whining. Teenagers do not have to be ashamed of such a hero."

After the play, the group of Elvis, Vera and their friends went to the Eve Bar, a nightclub in Munich at Karolinenplatz 2a, near the Amerikahaus institute. Accompanying the group were a gossip columnist, Anatol Aber, who wrote for *BRAVO* and *Quick* magazines, and a choreographer, Irene Mann. Playful pictures were taken of Elvis arm-wrestling with Irene at the Eve Bar.

At this point, Lamar and Red had been asked to leave the Tschechowa household. Vera's mom did not want them there anymore. She had "a very low opinion of Red and Lamar. She thought them rude and uncouth – specifically in their use of bad language, their raids on the refrigerator and they 'always had their feet on the table'." Coming home drunk did not help either.

As a result, Red and Lamar went to stay at the Hotel Edelweiss and Elvis would soon follow. According to separate accounts by Vera and her mother, Elvis got kicked out one night later, either for bothering their pets as Vera claimed, or for fooling around with Vera in the house, as her mother claimed. The practical reason which seems more likely is that the presence of fans waiting outside the house became too much to tolerate, so Elvis was asked to stay somewhere else.

However, Presley's move to a hotel did not end his friendship with Vera and her mother. On March 4, Vera took Elvis and his friends to the movies to see two of her films: *Under 18* and *The Doctor of Stalingrad*. Later that evening after Vera's play, Elvis met up with Vera and three friends of hers – German lyricist Walter Brandin, his wife, Elisabeth, and Toni Netzle, public relations manager for Polydor Records. Toni claims that Elvis said he wanted to go to a nightclub, so Walter suggested the Moulin Rouge.

The sophisticated club, known for its striptease shows and nighttime cabaret, was notified in advance that Elvis Presley would be coming. Once Elvis arrived, the club did not let anyone else in. As he and his entourage were seated at a table in the middle of the club, the band started playing Elvis Presley songs trying to get him to perform. Elvis tried to go onstage and sing, but Red and Lamar put a stop to that, since he was not allowed to perform in public while he was in the army, at the orders of Colonel Parker.

"One of his bodyguards said that he should stop – he should know that he is not allowed to sing – it is forbidden," recalled Toni Netzle. "Then he was singing at the table, and that wasn't allowed either. So, then he beat the time [on the table], and that wasn't allowed either."

Vera, Toni Netzle and Elisabeth Brandin were all surprised at how Elvis obediently did whatever his bodyguards told him to do. They observed how Red and Lamar would escort Elvis to the bathroom. If his hair was tousled, they would tell Elvis to comb his hair. If he wanted to toast with everyone with a glass of champagne, they would tell him to drink his tomato or orange juice instead.

Even though the press was kept in the dark about the visit, there were still a multitude of photographs taken that night. The Moulin Rouge had a house photographer, Rudolf Paulini, who took countless photos of Elvis at the club with fans and with the dancers who worked there. The existence of the photos was not revealed until 1978 when they were published in the book, *Private Elvis*.

Comparing these photos of Elvis to those he took with regular fans, the Moulin Rouge pictures seem a bit tawdry. Elvis happily posed with anyone who wanted a picture, but the dancers seemed to add an aggressive flair to their photos with The King of Rock and Roll by posing with a dramatic look on their faces or enticing Elvis to hold them in erotic ways.

For example, Elvis is photographed with twin showgirls, the Orkowskis, in seductive poses as he takes turns kissing one twin standing to his left as the other grabs and embraces him from his right side, and vice versa. Presley was also photographed with a stripper. She had multiple photos taken with Elvis after the show where she was kissing Elvis on the lips. In one photo, she was sticking out her tongue, trying to entice Elvis to do the same. It could have been another version of Presley's famous "Kiss" photo from 1956, but Elvis was not a willing participant.

Meanwhile, the question of where things stood between Elvis and his date of the evening, Vera, was looming. The couple appeared on covers of multiple publications in Germany and the U.S. publicizing a supposed romance. One magazine even falsely claimed that Elvis and Vera were secretly engaged and planning to marry. But was there any truth at all to the romance rumors?

"Elvis was after her, all right," confirmed Lamar. "That's why he stayed at her house."

It seems that Elvis was definitely interested in Vera, but the romance seemed to be one-sided. That night at the Moulin Rouge, Presley's prospects with Vera started to fade. Vera and her friends left early which allowed Elvis' attention to be diverted to the multiple women at the club. Red, Lamar and Elvis stayed until 4 a.m.

The next morning on March 5, Elvis went back to the Tschechowas house for breakfast. He had bits of tinsel in his hair and eyebrows and told Vera he had stayed at the club the whole night. Vera believed Elvis was interested in one of the dancers at the club. Observers believe it was a blonde dancer named Angelika Zehetbauer who he was also photographed with at the Moulin Rouge.

Elvis said goodbye to Vera after breakfast. He was due back at the end of the day to Friedberg, but reports say he and his friends went to the Moulin Rouge again, then returned to Friedberg in the early morning of March 6.

From Vera's point of view, her relationship with Elvis was purely for publicity purposes. As Red West explained: "That was all her (Vera's) mother. She was out for the publicity for her daughter. That's all it was – just publicity."

Vera appeared to have no emotional attachment to Elvis, but instead hoped for a professional relationship in the future. Her friendship with Elvis could be summed up by her statement: "We hope we'll be able to make films together in Hollywood." Tschechowa was even considered to appear in Presley's 1960 film, *G.I. Blues*, but after screening some of her movies, producer Hal Wallis decided she "wasn't right" for the role.

Elvis would return again to Munich and then on to Paris in June 1959, but he never saw Vera Tschechowa again. In later years, Vera did not remember her time with Elvis fondly. She expressed distaste for the publicity stunts and emphasized that she never had any romantic interest in Elvis.

In August 1960, Vera clarified her relationship with Elvis: "I've gotten tired of all the fantastic stuff they write about Elvis and me. It seems hard to get through with the truth. But there was no romance. I can say he is a pleasant boy, but I couldn't say any more because I didn't know him well enough. We have never been in love with each other."

In the Summer of 1959, Elvis was asked about his relationship with Vera. "Vera sure wasn't out to use me for her own publicity," Elvis explained. "I believe that the press chased us out of their own motivation. Vera is well known, after all, and our friendship couldn't possibly go unnoticed. Plus, you can't really expect Vera to run away from the photographers. After all, she is a young actress who has to take care of her career. And that's why it didn't work out. Unfortunately."

REPORT OF MEDICAL EXAMINATION

1. LAST NAME—FIRST NAME—MIDDLE NAME		2. GRADE AND COMPONENT OR POSITION	3. IDENTIFICATION NO.
PRESLEY, ELVIS ARON			
4. HOME ADDRESS (Number, street or RFD, city or town, zone and State)		5. PURPOSE OF EXAMINATION	6. DATE OF EXAMINATION
1034 Audubon Drive, Memphis, Tennessee		Preinduction	4 January 1957
7. SEX	8. RACE	9. TOTAL YRS. GOVT. SERVICE MILITARY / CIVILIAN	10. DEPARTMENT, AGENCY, OR SERVICE	11. ORGANIZATION UNIT
Male	Caucasian			
12. DATE OF BIRTH	13. PLACE OF BIRTH	14. NAME, RELATIONSHIP, AND ADDRESS OF NEXT OF KIN		
8 Jan 1935	Tupelo, Mississippi			
15. EXAMINING FACILITY OR EXAMINER, AND ADDRESS		16. OTHER INFORMATION		
AFES Memphis Tenn		SS# 40 86 35 16		

17. RATING OR SPECIALTY

CLINICAL EVALUATION			NOTES.—Describe every abnormality in detail. (Enter pertinent item number before each comment; continue in item 73 and use additional sheets if necessary.)
NORMAL	ABNOR- MAL	(Check each item in appropriate column; enter "N.E." if not evaluated)	
X		18. HEAD, FACE, NECK, AND SCALP	
X		19. NOSE	
X		20. SINUSES	
X		21. MOUTH AND THROAT	
X		22. EARS—GENERAL (Int. & ext. canals) (Auditory acuity under items 39 and 71)	
X		23. DRUMS (Perforation)	
X		24. EYES—GENERAL (Visual acuity and refraction under items 55, 56, and 57)	
X	-	25. OPHTHALMOSCOPIC	

On January 4, 1957 just days before his 22nd birthday,
Elvis went for his preinduction army physical in Memphis.

Goodbye, Mom

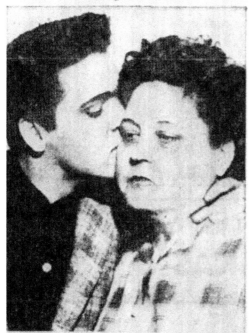

Preparing to enter the Army, singer Elvis Presley
kisses his mother at home in Memphis. Tenn., yes-

The Presleys welcomed the press into Graceland on March 23, 1958, the night before Elvis got inducted into the army. Elvis was worried about leaving his mother. The stress Gladys Presley felt about her only son being drafted added to her growing physical ailments.
[*Bristol Daily Courier* (PA), 3/24/58]

85

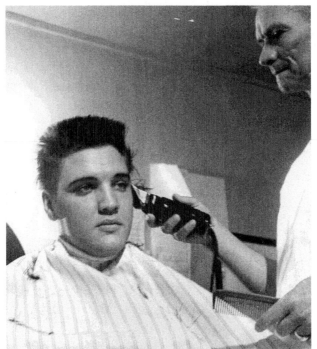

Elvis had two pre-army haircuts before his legendary clipping, but there was still a lot of hair to trim off! [Bob Klein Media]

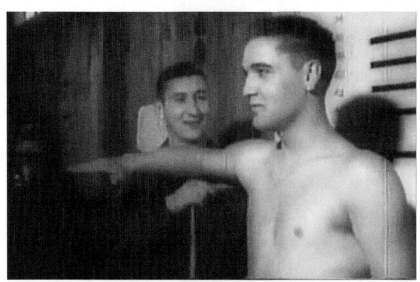

Colonel Parker made sure to it that every aspect of Elvis' induction into the army got covered by the press.

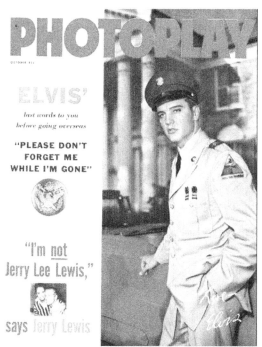

Photos taken at Graceland in June 1958 while Elvis was on leave were used to keep Presley's name in the limelight in magazines like *Photoplay* (10/58).

Kitty Dolan shared her story about being involved with Elvis and visiting him at his rented home in Killeen, TX in magazines like *Elvis in the Army*.

PRESLEY GOES OVERSEAS—Rock 'n' roll singer Elvis Presley bends ove the railing to kiss one of his fans, Lillian Portnoy,

Fan Lillian Portnoy got a kiss from Elvis as his ship was leaving New York. The photo appeared in many papers across the country (9/23/58).

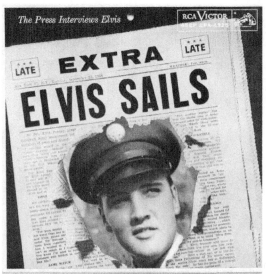

Elvis interviews from the September 1958 press conference in Brooklyn were released by RCA on an EP.

by MARGRIT BUERGIN

age 17, Frankfurt, Germany
(as told to Jean Lewis)

For many months after Elvis started dating Margit Buergin in Germany, she received a great amount of attention from the media. [Pictured: "Elvis Kissed Me" in *Photoplay* (3/59)].

Elvis took publicity photos with German actress, Vera Tschechowa, in early 1959. Many publications fabricated a false love affair between them.

Fans love to recreate this photo from the 45 record sleeve for
"A Big Hunk O' Love" taken in Bad Nauheim.

The 1959 Christmas card sent out by Colonel Parker used two
photos of Elvis taken during his spring photo shoot in Bad Nauheim.

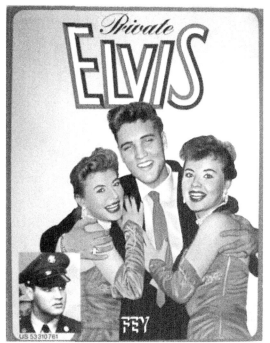

Photos taken from Presley's first visit to Munich are featured
in the book, *Private Elvis* by Diego Cortez. The book shows some
provocative photos of Elvis with dancers and strippers.

In August 1959, Elvis sits with teenagers at Hattsteinweiher Lake.
[Credit: Dr. Peter Weidemann, Wikimedia Commons, cropped]

A FAREWELL LETTER TO ELVIS—With his picture on the table in front of her, Priscilla Beaulieu, 16, writes a letter to Elvis Presley. Priscilla, of Austin, Texas, is the daughter of a U.S.

A few days after Elvis left Germany, Priscilla Beaulieu posed for pictures for the media which appeared in papers across the U.S. (3/5/60)

Welcome home, Elvis!
Elvis answers questions from the press at Fort Dix, NJ
on the day he returned home to the U.S. on March 3, 1960.

15

QUESTIONING HIS DUTY TO SERVE

After the excitement of visiting Munich and the Moulin Rouge, it was back to reality for Elvis. His battalion was due for another field training maneuver in Grafenwoehr that month. Lieutenant Bill Taylor interacted often with Presley's platoon during that trip in March 1959 and spent a good deal of time with Elvis.

One day when they were out on the field together, Elvis and Lt. Taylor got a chance to have an in-depth conversation. They talked about how the U.S. military was facing a threat from the Soviet Union over the divided city of Berlin referred to as the "Berlin crisis." Western countries were trying to support the border staying open between East Germany and West Germany, while the U.S.S.R. wanted the border closed. The reality was that if tensions escalated, the U.S. army could be called into combat at any time.

It was the height of the Cold War with the U.S.S.R. expanding their power around the world. Just two years after Elvis and Lt. Taylor had this discussion in Grafenwoehr, the Berlin Wall would be constructed.

The conversation between Presley and Taylor then expanded to war in general, what the soldiers were fighting for, and the reasons the U.S. fought in World War II compared to The Korean War. Presley seemed to agree with U.S. involvement in World War II, but not the conflict in Korea.

"Most people I know don't want any more Korean war kind of stuff," Presley told Lt. Taylor. "I mean goin' around the world and gettin' killed because some politician wants to show how tough he is."

What prompted this statement was most likely the fact that Presley's cousin, Carol "Junior" Smith, had served in the Korean War which ended in 1953. Junior, who was a few years older than Elvis, and his younger brother, Gene Smith, would accompany Elvis on tour in the early days of

Presley's career from 1956 to when Elvis joined the army. However, Junior had been traumatized from the combat he experienced in Korea. He suffered from "shell shock" - what is now known as PTSD or post-traumatic stress disorder. As a result, Junior started drinking heavily and exhibiting strange and odd behavior that was evident to many of Presley's friends. Junior Smith ended up dying of alcohol poisoning at the age of 28 on February 4, 1961.

"He [Junior] was sullen and disturbed because of what had happened to him when he was in the army in Korea," explained Presley's younger cousin, Billy Smith. "I remember him as a fun-loving guy... He had his expressions and he even had a bad eye like [actor Jack] Elam. Elam always looked like he was about to do something really painful to you. So did Junior! Junior was at my house in my bed when he died."

Elvis was lucky that he just missed getting drafted for the Korean war. When he registered for the draft in January 1953, the war was still being fought with the United States troops supporting South Korea against the totalitarian regime in North Korea. Usually, young men could expect to be drafted one year after graduating from high school. At the time, Gladys was distraught thinking that her only son might be placed in danger.

However, a month after Presley's high school graduation, a truce was signed between North Korea and South Korea. As a result, the army then had a surplus of men serving, so men who registered for the draft in 1953 like Elvis were not called to serve until several years later.

Elvis told Lt. Taylor that many people back home did not understand why he chose to serve as a regular soldier. At the very least, Elvis knew he could handle it because he had some experience with the military before being drafted. He grew up with a background in the JROTC (Junior Reserve Officer Training Corps) program at high school which would serve him well in the army.

During a press conference before he left the U.S. for Germany, Presley was asked by a reporter if his high school JROTC experience helped him so far as a soldier. Elvis gave a sarcastic answer: "Yes ma'am, it definitely did. I knew my left leg from my right one and it helped quite a bit (laughs)."

All kidding aside, having been in the JROTC surely helped prepare Elvis for army service. Many entertainers who were drafted avoided the nitty-gritty duties as a soldier and would serve in public relations or entertainment posts. In fact, the same time Elvis was serving, a British rock and roll singer, Terry Dene, was drafted in the U.K. Unlike Elvis, he did not fare well. He could not handle the army lifestyle and had to be admitted to the hospital for mental stress. After two months, he received a medical discharge, with military doctors claiming he was "unfit to be a soldier."

At age 15, Elvis started 10th grade by enrolling in the JROTC. His friend George Klein also joined. High school students who participate in the JROTC are not required to join the military after high school. These youth training and development programs are taught by retired service members. The goal of the programs is to teach good citizenship through coursework on military history and participation in community service. Members are usually required to wear a uniform once a week to school and to JROTC events.

Red West, who went to high school with Elvis, said "Elvis was constantly getting demerits for not having a haircut. He was always doing extra duty and he only took the required two years, while the rest of us went on to become officers in our third year."

Even though Elvis may have had a hard time adhering to the JROTC rules, George Klein said "it was Elvis' ROTC days in high school that enabled him to become a squad leader while in basic training" in Fort Hood.

In addition, the JROTC gave Elvis a connection to starting his musical career. Mildred Scrivener was Presley's senior class homeroom teacher at Humes High School. As a retired Lieutenant Colonel, she also served as the ROTC sponsor at the school. Scrivener was a producer of the Humes annual Minstrel Show on April 9, 1953 which helped give Elvis the confidence to pursue a singing career from the enthusiastic reception he received from his fellow students.

"We agreed that only one encore would be given – by the act that got the most applause," Scrivener recalled. "When [Elvis] finished, there was thunderous applause. It was Elvis who gave the encore for us all. He was so pleased that he rushed off the stage and flung his arms around my neck. 'They like me!' he shouted."

"Mrs. Scrivener was responsible for urging Elvis on," recalled Presley's classmate, Sue Wing (formerly Sue Shelton), "even getting him on stage. We really had a preview of rock 'n' roll as Elvis was in a couple of school shows and was a hit."

Never forgetting where he came from, Elvis went to visit Mrs. Scrivener at Humes along with buddy, Nick Adams, after becoming a star. He had just returned from Hollywood having completed filming of *Love Me Tender*. As a result of his visit on September 24, 1956, he wrote a $900 check to Humes for new uniforms for the JROTC program. When Elvis went into the army, the Humes JROTC gave him an old musket as a going-away present.

Nevertheless, two years participating in the JROTC did not mean Elvis necessarily wanted to serve in the military. However, he did briefly consider enlisting when he first got out of high school: "I might have been in uniform before this if my mother hadn't wanted me to wait for the draft," Elvis said.

Even though Elvis did not speak out against being drafted and seemed content to go along with it, in private he did not support the draft. He told his friend Alan Fortas who considered enlisting so he could serve with Elvis: "I gotta go and I'm goin'. But I'll tell you one thing. Make 'em come get you. Don't join anything. Take your chances."

In fact, Elvis publicly supported a Presidential candidate who wanted to get rid of the draft. In 1956, the first year that he was eligible to vote for President, Presley was quoted as supporting Adlai Stevenson. Stevenson was the Democratic candidate running against the Republican incumbent, Dwight D. "Ike" Eisenhower.

"I'm strictly for Stevenson," Elvis proclaimed, as reported in the September 10, 1956 issue of *Time* magazine. "I don't dig the intellectual bit, but I'm telling you, man, he knows the most."

A few times, Elvis let it slip out to reporters how he personally felt about being drafted. In August 1956 when Elvis was in St. Petersburg, Florida, he told a reporter that he had not heard from the Memphis draft board in the three years since he registered, "and I hope I never do," he added.

Nevertheless, Elvis did exceptionally well while he served in the army. He rose from private to sergeant in much less time than most draftees. And most importantly, he gained respect among his fellow soldiers and higher-ranking officers.

Meanwhile, the army was still trying to get Elvis to serve in more of a public relations type of role. While he was in Grafenwoehr, the army made him an offer to go on a publicity tour. According to Presley's friend, Charlie Hodge, the army told Elvis: "We're going to take you to Miami to a disc jockey convention and then we're gonna take you to Paris to the Air Show and then we've made arrangements for you to meet the Pope."

It was a tempting offer since at the time Elvis was in the field sleeping in three feet of snow. But after consulting with Colonel Parker, Elvis declined saying: "I just can't leave these 40,000 men... and then come back and start working with them again after they've been sleeping in the snow and I've been to all those beautiful places. I think I'll just stay and drive my jeep and do my job."

Myrlen Britt, who served in Germany the same time as Elvis, recalled seeing Presley on duty standing in a snowstorm as he guided M59 tanks into parking spaces. "I never met Presley, but he had a great reputation [as a soldier] among others who knew him," said Britt.

"Presley was cold, he was wet, and he was ankle deep in the snow, like everyone else," said the commanding officer of the 5th Corps, Lieutenant-General FW Farrell.

"He [Elvis] has fooled us all," said a U.S. Army senior commander in Frankfurt. "We had our stomach full of these celebrities, singers, and so on, and we figured Presley for just another kleig-light eight-ball... (but) he's never angled himself into anything easy, and he shows exceptionally good judgment for a kid worth a few million dollars. Elvis has made it popular to be a good soldier. It's great for us. We'd like to keep him in the army."

After returning from this two-week field training at Grafenwoehr, Elvis was approaching his one-year mark of having served in the army in late March 1959. To celebrate, his friends threw him an "Over the Hump" party on March 27. The party seemed to be instigated by Colonel Parker all the way from the States. The party banner that was displayed on the wall showed a caricature of The Colonel pushing Elvis sitting in a car on the path to his future army release. One year down, one more to go!

16

SECRET ROCK AND ROLL MANEUVERS

Everywhere Elvis went, he was asked to sing – whether it be in the army barracks, at parties with his fellow G.I.s, or in nightclubs in Munich and Paris. Technically, he was not allowed to sing in public while serving in the army – at least that is what he told people. He blamed it on his record contract with RCA which he said forbid him to perform during his military service. But most likely, the edict had come from Colonel Parker who did not want Elvis to sing in public without getting paid.

However, for someone so passionate about music like Elvis, it was hard for him to adhere to that rule. In fact, there were several times while Presley was in the army that he performed in private settings that the public was unaware of. Only through eyewitness accounts that have come out over the years have we learned of exclusive concerts given for the lucky few in Germany by The King of Rock and Roll.

For example, one day while on duty, Elvis and Sgt. Ira Jones were taking a coffee break at the mess hall at Ray Barracks. Next door was the Non-Commissioned Officers (NCO) Club. Elvis was in the mood to sing and he asked Sgt. Jones if there was a piano in the club. Jones said there was. Presley then asked if Jones could take him in there while they were on their short break.

Even though the club was closed at the time, Jones had access because he was an official of the club. Elvis walked up to the piano situated on a small stage facing the dance floor. The club was empty except for a German cleaning lady scrubbing the edge of the hardwood floor.

Sgt. Jones quickly became mesmerized as Elvis started playing the piano and singing a private mini-concert to an empty room. The King of Rock and Roll was fired up and he played hit after hit, with a love ballad and a gospel song thrown in between his signature rock and roll songs. Elvis sang for 15 minutes.

The cleaning lady stood frozen as she realized the magic she had just witnessed. Tears came to her eyes as she went over and asked Elvis to sign his autograph on a scrap of paper she found in her pocket. Elvis was so touched by her emotion that he "raised her face and kissed the tears from her eyes." Without saying a word, "he patted her shoulder gently and made his exit."

Sgt. Jones was so choked up that he had to take a moment to himself to hide the waves of emotion he felt having just watched a superstar perform before his very eyes. Jones thought to himself that he and this lucky woman, who happened to be in the right place at the right time, had just been given a free concert which millions of fans would have paid to see.

That special mini concert at the NCO Club was just the beginning. Since Elvis spent so much time driving Sgt. Jones around in his jeep, the Sergeant witnessed Elvis singing on many occasions, frequently while driving together in the jeep and sometimes around other soldiers. Presley and Jones would often harmonize together since Jones was a singer himself.

After returning from maneuvers in Grafenwoehr in the Spring of 1959, both Sgt. Jones and Lt. Bill Taylor were getting ready to leave Germany. They had both been reassigned to new posts back in the States. As a result, the platoon decided to have a farewell party for their leader, Sgt. Jones, in early April 1959.

For the party to remain private, they chose a location off the beaten track at a lesser-known "gasthaus," or small German inn, called Herrnmühle restaurant so that the fans would not find out. All the soldiers were welcome to bring their wives or girlfriends. Elvis brought Margit Buergin.

Halfway through the party, Elvis offered to sing. He walked over to the piano and sang his hits like "All Shook Up," "Heartbreak Hotel," "Don't Be Cruel," "Love Me Tender" and "That's When Your Heartaches Begin." He also dedicated "Hound Dog" to Lt. Taylor, who he called "Wild Bill" at the party. The restaurant staff could not believe their eyes!

"I thought the Gasthaus would explode," described Lt. Taylor. "Everyone, especially the girls, went crazy. The waitresses, the hausfrau (wives), the maintenance men, and the dishwashers all came out to watch… [they] cheered as if their hometown football team had pulled the biggest upset in the world. They were ecstatic!"

Elvis played for an hour. After his performance, Elvis presented the Sergeant with a beautiful watch. He also had gifts made up for all the guests including men's and women's leather wallets with "EP" stamped in the leather. Lt. Taylor and his wife were impressed at how Elvis made a point of talking to everyone at the party.

"I can't believe that you two are both leavin'," Elvis told Lt. Taylor. "You two have been very important to me. Swear to God, if you hadn't been around, my days would have been a lot different. I really appreciate the time you took when I wanted to talk."

Lt. Taylor was deeply moved by Presley's words. When Elvis told Taylor that he would not forget him, Taylor replied the same. That was the last time he would ever see Elvis.

A few days later, Sgt. Jones saw Elvis and his platoon for the last time. "I have become accustomed to ducking fans, to hearing you sing, and to the platoon being the center of all the attention you have brought it," Sgt. Jones told Elvis as he bid his platoon good-bye. "I will miss you and I will be lost in my next assignment… I've never had so much fun in all my life."

One feature that Presley's secret concerts shared is that no photographs or tangible proof of the performances exist. The only account that exists are from the eyewitnesses who were there – including those who were at the most surprising secret concert that Elvis did in Germany at the Micky Bar in Grafenwoehr in December 1958.

It is quite shocking that this concert took place because not only was the show a secret, but so was the fact that Elvis had been staying at the apartment above the Micky Bar for close to a week while he was on maneuvers. While on the surface, it may have seemed outlandish for the army to permit this, the prospect makes sense once you understand the circumstances surrounding Presley's presence in Grafenwoehr.

While Elvis put up a brave face in front of his commanding officers and fellow troops during field maneuvers, he was miserable in the cold weather. In fact, in private, Elvis expressed his displeasure with the training environment in two letters he wrote in November 1958. In a letter to Sgt. Bill Norwood, the commanding officer who he befriended in Fort Hood, Elvis said:

"We are up at a place called Grafenwoehr. I'm sure you've heard of it. It's miserable up here and we are here for six weeks. The German people are very nice and friendly, but there is no place like the good ole U.S. I am with a bunch of boys and Sgts., although I would have given anything to stay at Ft. Hood with you guys."

In another letter he wrote to his friend, Alan Fortas, back in Memphis, Elvis said: "You know I am bound to be pretty lonely or I wouldn't be writing a letter. We are up at a training area for 50 days and believe me it's miserable. It's cold and there is nothing at all to do up here." Elvis ended the letter by saying, "Well, I gotta go wade in the mud."

Presley was also still grieving over his mother's death. Elisabeth Stefaniak said that when she met Elvis that November in Grafenwoehr, he would often talk about his mother and start crying. It was even reported that he was calling his father, Vernon, back in Bad Nauheim every day. Technically, Elvis was not permitted to bring anyone with him on these maneuvers including Lamar, Red or his father because he was supposed to be sleeping on location in the field or at the camp.

Elvis had a lot of time on his hands while he was on these reconnaissance, or scouting, training missions in the field near the border of Czechoslovakia. In fact, one source claimed: "Eyewitness accounts (by teenage observers) are reporting, that Elvis really liked to meet up with German people at nearby farm houses. Especially because it was warmer and more comfortable inside a building than outside on the fields."

However, Presley was stationed there for six weeks from November 3, 1959 to December 16, 1959. That was a long time for Elvis to be away from his family – not to mention it was a long time to be out on a training ground along with thousands of other soldiers. As a result, he was becoming a spectacle out in the field. Other officers were constantly trying to get access to him. As reported in the army magazine *Stars & Stripes*: "Most maneuvering took place around Elvis, than at any other place in the fields."

Add to that the fact that even though there was a press ban inside the grounds, the press was still going to great lengths to track Presley's every move on this trip. As a result, it would not be surprising if Elvis was given undisclosed approval to find a way to escape during the last week of maneuvers.

"When no one was watching, he [Elvis] was able to get some special treatments," explained Rex Mansfield. "His special treatment was handled on a very discreet, low key basis and the people who knew really didn't mind. If things were a little slow, he could slip out and go home for a while. There were no big favors handed to him, just a lot of small ones that nobody would really fuss about."

According to local resident Raimund Rodler, Presley's battalion commander contacted Rodler's mother and stepfather, Margarete and Alter Feiner, the owners of the Micky Bar, whom he knew through their jukebox repair business. The army commander told them that Presley's father, Vernon, was coming to Grafenwoehr, but since he was not allowed to stay with Elvis at the camp, they needed a place for Vernon to stay where he would not be disturbed. They offered Vernon the upstairs furnished apartment with a bedroom, a large living room and a winter garden.

As a result, Vernon Presley came up to Grafenwoehr for almost a week in December and stayed in the guest quarters above the Micky Bar. That allowed Elvis to secretly come there every night and stay with his father. He had a taxi driver take him back to Camp Algiers in the Grafenwoehr training area each morning. Surprisingly, Elvis got out of the house every day without the staff noticing since he was picked up at the back entrance, and then brought back to that same spot in the evening. The only ones that knew he was there were the owners.

While Elvis was at the camp during the day, Vernon accompanied Raimund to work fixing jukeboxes: "Twice he came with me to repair some jukeboxes," explained Raimund. "It was great fun for him. Of course, I had him play his son's songs then."

Mrs. Feiner offered home-cooked meals for Elvis and Vernon. Her specialty was schnitzel sandwiches (pork fried in butter). Elvis loved her sandwiches and "wanted schnitzel with fried potatoes every day." Mrs. Feiner would even pack some for Elvis to take with him to the camp for duty.

"We had breakfast together, we had dinner together, we played cards with each other," explained Rodler. "Elvis was so casual, so uncomplicated - no star. He was a star, but he did not act like that."

It is believed that Elvis performed the secret Micky Bar concert on one of the last few days that he was in Grafenwoehr, probably somewhere between December 12 and 15, 1958. The concert came about as a thank you from Presley to the Feiner family. Margarete refused to take any money from the Presleys for their visit, so Elvis said he would do a surprise private concert in the afternoon exclusively for the 30-person staff of the Micky Bar before the bar opened that day for business. However, he would perform on the condition that no photographs and no recordings would be permitted, and that no strangers be allowed in.

The Micky Bar, originally called the "Mönchshof", was the perfect place for a secret Elvis concert. It was built in 1954 and would host live music every day. They had a house band of six or seven musicians, as well as various performers including magicians, singers and striptease artists. It could hold up to 400 people and was popular with Germans as well as American soldiers, who gave the bar its adopted name.

On the day of Presley's concert, the staff was told to come at half past two, but they did not know for what reason. Once all the staff had arrived, the management locked the door and Elvis came down the stairs to the stage. To the staff's delight, he played the piano and sang for two and a half hours just for them.

Waitress Pauline Neubert was confused. She saw this soldier come in and start playing the piano and singing, but she did not know who he was. She went and asked Mrs. Feiner, "Who is the one playing so nicely?" Mrs. Feiner replied: "Elvis Presley - *The* Elvis Presley!"

When Elvis would sing spontaneously for the boys in the barracks, he would usually sing old folk songs like "I'll Take You Home Again, Kathleen." Either out of modesty or to avoid the possibility of someone recording him which might cause trouble with RCA, he would avoid singing his own records. However, at the secret Micky Bar concert, he played his own rock and roll songs. It truly was a memorable show for the exclusive German audience!

"Elvis sang without a microphone," recalled Rodler decades later. "Almost all of his hits were there. I can remember 'Hound Dog' and 'Love Me Tender' for nearly fifty years. These were nice hours. Between the songs, Elvis, the world star, talked to the staff." Describing Elvis as "young and shy" during the performance, Rodler said the audience "enjoyed the two hours without screeching and fainting, because most were already around 30 years old."

After the concert, Elvis left Grafenwoehr, but the news of the gig spread like wildfire. Many fans came to the Micky Bar in hopes of seeing Elvis, but he had already gone. Presley left knowing that he had fulfilled his desire to give back to his German hosts who had been so gracious to him and his father.

"Afterwards, he [Elvis] called us two or three times," recalled Rodler. "He said thank you and invited us to [Bad] Nauheim. And then I got an invitation to America. Everything would have been free of charge - the flight, the hotel, everything free. But my wife was a bit under the weather at that time and I did not want to go alone, so I stayed. I called him – doesn't work."

Rodler said that they had their own pictures from the concert, but when his mother died in 1991, his stepfather threw them all away. Also, after his mother's death, Rodler said they put the Micky Bar piano that Elvis played at the concert in storage. A few years later, they lent it to the nearby Hotel Rußweiher in Eschenbach where it was displayed in the foyer of the hotel for 20 years.

In 2016, the grand piano that Elvis played that night was moved to The Culture and Military Museum of Grafenwoehr. There stands the memory of one of the few secret concerts that Elvis performed in Germany.

17

A LEGENDARY PHOTO

Colonel Parker's influence could be felt in Germany in the spring of 1959 when he sent photographer Don Cravens there to do an exclusive photo shoot with Elvis. In a letter dated March 23, 1959, Colonel Parker explained to Elvis why they desperately needed professional photos taken to promote Presley's army image. The Colonel was not happy with the multitude of photos in newspapers and magazines that were circulating out of Germany at this time. These photos did not play into the image that the Colonel wanted Elvis to project.

"Most of the photos being when you are off duty and they all look like all you have to do is autograph and visit with fans - at least that is the way they come out in the magazines," wrote Colonel Parker. "The kids are writing in that they are tired looking at the same type of photos of Elvis from Germany with the German girl, with Anita Wood, with Kitty Dolan and others. I know that you can't help this and I know that you appreciate me getting something done about trying to get something new and refreshing going. This is one reason why I hired Mr. Craven on our own so that we can get something rolling..."

Don Cravens was a photographer for *LIFE* magazine. Not only did he take some iconic photos of Presley in earlier years while he was on assignment, but he also was hired as a freelancer by The Colonel, who he became friends with. It was Cravens who took the beautiful color portrait of Elvis in uniform with his parents in June 1958 when he came home on leave from the army. Those family photos would be the last pictures that Elvis took with his mother before her death.

In late March/early April 1959, Cravens flew over to Germany to do the photo shoot with Elvis. Although it was supposed to be a well-kept secret, one newspaper, *The Nashville Banner*, printed a blurb about it: "It's supposed to be hush-hush, but *LIFE* magazine lensman Don Cravens, who lives in Nashville, has been in Germany where he shot jillion photographs of Army's Elvis Presley...And they said it couldn't be done."

Cravens apparently spent a month in Germany with Elvis. He recalled his experience years later: "I hated to go to breakfast with Elvis," Cravens said in a 1986 interview. "His grandmother was there with him, and two or three cronies – the 'Memphis Mafia.' She cooked great rashers of bacon, and he would take the toast and soak it in the bacon grease and eat it – and that made me sick. But Elvis would insist; so I had fried eggs swimming in bacon grease, with mounds of toast."

Cravens said that Elvis was not that eager to do the photo shoot. "It was hard to get him to stay still," Cravens continued. "I'd tell Elvis: 'The Colonel's going to raise hell.' And Elvis would answer: 'Don't worry about it. He hasn't called me yet.'"

What many fans would consider to be the most iconic photos of Elvis in Germany were taken that spring. There were four different scenes shown in these photos taken in Bad Nauheim: Elvis posing on a bridge, Elvis posing in front of an archway, Elvis posing with horses and Elvis posing with a German Shepherd.

Not much is known about the photo shoot. What can be deduced from looking at the assortment of photos is that Elvis decided to walk around the town of Bad Nauheim and the photographer would spontaneously decide what would be good locations for photographs. The weather appeared to be overcast. Some believe that it must have been done on a Sunday because there were not many people walking around.

One shot shows Elvis walking by a restaurant called Gasthaus Zur Krone. Elvis is most likely heading around the corner towards the archway, known as the Burgpforte, or Castle Gate. The memorable shot of Elvis leaning against the wall of a building shows the Castle Gate in the background. Elvis is photographed in a few different poses including with his whole back against the wall, and his face staring in different directions.

This picturesque shot captured the look of old-fashioned European architecture as a backdrop for this most handsome Hollywood star in uniform. The photo of Elvis leaning with just his shoulder against the wall and looking towards the camera was chosen to be the cover photo for his new 45 rpm single of "A Big Hunk O' Love" released in the States in June 1959. The single would hit number one and sell half a million copies in the U.S. Since then, that photo became a popular one to be recreated by Elvis fans, and there is now a framed marker about the Elvis photo on the building near the archway.

Another series of shots depicts Elvis posing with horses in front of the Dankeskirche church (the "Thanksgiving" church). It just so happens that a horse-drawn carriage was sitting in front of the church at the time. Presley, who had a love for horseback riding, went up to the horses and petted them as the photographer took several shots.

Then, on the grounds near the church, it appears that Elvis and Vernon randomly encountered a man and his German Shepherd. Elvis was then photographed petting the German Shepherd from multiple angles. The identity of the man is not known, although he was photographed casually standing and talking with Vernon and Elvis that day. Those were the days when the biggest rock and roll star in the world could walk around and take pictures in a small European town and not be bothered.

For some more picturesque photos, Elvis posed on two different bridges. The first bridge he posed on had a waist-high cement barrier that he leaned against. Those photos have only appeared in black and white. There are a series of small pedestrian and traffic bridges that line up with each other crossing the Usa river in Bad Nauheim. Since this first bridge was located so close to other bridges, it displayed a busy background with people and cars in the shots. As a result, Elvis and his photographer were probably not happy with the look of the images, so they walked over to take more photos at a more secluded bridge.

The second bridge had a fancy metal railing and was further removed from the other bridges. This is where the classic color photo of Elvis leaning against the railing with a backdrop of beautiful scenery was taken. The first bridge can be seen in the far distant background. It became a classic photo which portrayed the mood of "Elvis the Soldier" alone in Germany on a somber day with nothing else surrounding him but trees and water under the bridge, as the saying goes.

Colonel Parker was quite happy with the photos and made good use of three of them. He used the images (with the background removed) of Elvis petting the German Shepherd, and also Elvis standing with the horses on the official Elvis Christmas card for 1959. The photo of Elvis near the archway used on the "A Big Hunk O' Love" single was also used as a publicity photo in magazines. That same photo of Elvis appeared in the

February 1960 issue of *Photoplay* magazine for their "calendar" of celebrity photos.

Presley looked so handsome and professional posing in his green army uniform. But behind the scenes, it took a lot of effort for Elvis to look so good. Presley was meticulous about his uniforms. He bought multiple pairs of boots and had Lamar Fike "spit-shine" them. He also bought multiple uniforms, shirts and pants and had Lamar and Red West take them to be cleaned and pressed on a regular basis – an advantage few of his fellow G.I.s had. Rex Mansfield revealed that Elvis would wear two-inch lifts in his shoes to appear taller, and George Klein said he sent Elvis the latest innovation in self-tanning from the States called Man Tan that Elvis started using towards the end of his stay in Germany. As a result, Presley was named "Best-Dressed Soldier" several times during his military service.

This series of photos taken in Bad Nauheim have proven over time to be the quintessential photos of Private Presley in Germany. Just like Beatles fans travel to the famous pedestrian crossing in London to recreate the iconic *Abbey Road* album cover, countless Elvis fans have made the journey to Bad Nauheim to recreate Presley's iconic photographs, specifically the cover photo of the "A Big Hunk O' Love" single. Similar to the photo of the four Beatles walking across the street in front of the Abbey Road recording studio, here was a photo taken in a public location, outside and accessible to everyone, enabling Elvis fans to easily recreate the picture.

Additionally, the photo of Elvis leaning on the bridge railing is so popular that it has now been permanently recreated with the creation of a bronze statue. The town of Bad Nauheim reconstructed the "Elvis bridge" in 2021 for the statue with new decorative railings that replicate the original ones that were in place in 1959. The Elvis bronze statue, which is scheduled to be unveiled in August 2021, is a life-size three-dimensional rendering of Elvis posing on the bridge that Spring day in 1959. Now Elvis fans from around the world can pose with Elvis while he was in the army!

18

GIRLS! GIRLS! AND KIDNAPPERS?

If anyone felt sorry for Elvis Presley being lonely and isolated in a small town in Germany, they needn't be worried. Elvis had his choice of many girls to date during his off-duty time. There were so many, it was hard to keep track. At least, that's how Presley's live-in secretary and secret girlfriend, Elisabeth Stefaniak, saw it. Not to mention the fact that she could hear Elvis with other girls through the wall of her room.

"There would be at least a couple of girls each week, more on weekends," Elisabeth described. "These were often very beautiful girls [but] although I resented them, I knew they were not staying. I was… He never apologized. I guess he never felt he owed me an explanation."

Eighteen-year-old Jane Wilbanks, or "Janie," was still in the picture. She had been in Germany since December 1958 and dated Elvis off and on for the next ten months. During that time, she got to know the private side of Elvis, but claimed that their relationship was "innocent." Jane revealed that while he was in Germany, Elvis was worried about losing his hair "because of a rumor then that German weather made people go bald."

While continuing to spend time with Elvis at his Bad Nauheim house, Jane ended up becoming friends with Elisabeth. They would cook together, and spend time talking with Minnie Mae, or "Grandma," as they called her, in her bedroom. Grandma would tell them about her relatives from Mississippi, which is also where Jane was from.

"Our friendship really surprised me," Elisabeth revealed years later. "After all, she was my chief competition for the time being. I think Janie and I realized we were just two of the many girls vying for Elvis' attention, and accepting that fact of life brought us much closer."

When Janie returned to the States in September 1959, she was quoted by the Associated Press in a newspaper article declaring there was no romance between her and Elvis, and that he was not dating anyone special in Germany. However, years later, she acknowledged that their relationship leaned towards romance.

"I dated Elvis just like I did other people," Janie explained in 1986. "Of course, he was famous and that makes it different. But was he in love with me? No, I don't think so. But only Elvis could answer that."

Meanwhile, Elisabeth also got to know Margit Buergin, who Elvis dated from October 1958 through the spring of 1959. Since Margit did not speak much English, Elisabeth had to serve as interpreter for Elvis, much to her disgust.

"It was an awkward position Elvis had put me in," Elisabeth confessed. "He was the man I adored, and the last thing I was interested in was helping their relationship blossom. A few times I was tempted to tell Margit that Elvis said he wanted to call the whole thing off and don't ever come back."

Elvis told Elisabeth that he would not have sexual intercourse with her. He told her that he didn't do that with any girl that "he was going to see on a regular basis," because he couldn't risk getting her pregnant. But they still shared a bed almost every night. "He would sometimes just give me a good-night kiss and go to sleep," said Elisabeth. "It was like a comfort thing for him."

One afternoon, Elisabeth and Minnie Mae looked out the windows from the second floor of the house to see four young girls arrive for their own private "date" with Elvis. They were the lucky winners of a contest with the theme of "Have a cup of tea with Elvis!" sponsored by Star Revue magazine in Germany.

On Sunday, April 19, 1959, the winning entourage descended upon Presley's home in Bad Nauheim where he agreed to meet with them, sign autographs and have a chat with them over tea, or Pepsi-Cola as Elvis preferred. Their travel arrangements to Bad Nauheim and their hotel accommodations were all paid for by *Star Revue*.

That day, the girls were accompanied by a press agent from Paramount, his wife, a *Star Revue* photographer, and the editor of the magazine, Eva Windmöller, who would act as interpreter. There were three winners of the contest from the German cities of Detmold, Hamburg and Heilbronn. The winner from Detmold, Rosemarie Kiel, had polio, so she was permitted to bring a friend with her on the trip to help her get around. This created a group of four young women.

On their way to the meeting, which took place after lunchtime, the girls strolled through Bad Nauheim and purchased some flowers to present to Presley's grandmother. As they approached the house, they noticed all the blinds were closed on the first level. The wooden fence outside the house was covered in handwritten graffiti from fans, with messages like "Kiss me" and "I love you."

Red West opened the door and invited them into the living room. Rosemarie noticed a tape recorder and amplifier in one corner, and a piano with a guitar lying on top of it in another corner. Lamar Fike came out and played Elvis records for the group. They were permitted to look into a closet which was full of boxes of fan mail. Rosemarie spotted two guitars in another closet. While they were waiting for Elvis, Vernon came out and talked with them about the car accident he had recently been in a few weeks earlier.

Finally, Elvis came out and greeted them. He was wearing a grey plaid blazer with a maroon tie. He accepted the flowers for his grandmother and placed one in his lapel. Initially, Rosemarie noticed that Elvis started blushing when he saw the girls.

"I couldn't believe it," Rosemarie described. "It was incomprehensible to me. Such a big star blushed and was embarrassed! From this moment on, Elvis was my hero."

He invited the girls to sit down at a table in the living room next to the piano. Although he did not sing for them, Elvis offered them all Pepsi Cola. He chatted with them about his childhood and how he loved gospel music. He described his secret visits to local movie theaters and how he always had to leave early to avoid being recognized.

"While he was talking, he laughed so much that we were soon caught by his good mood," recalled Rosemarie. "We had a good time at Elvis' side. His whole behavior was so impressive."

When it was Rosemarie's turn to stand up and walk next to Elvis to get his autograph, she slipped since her walking stick was not in reach. As a result, she pulled the tablecloth down with her and the Pepsi bottles spilled, not only on her dress, but also on Presley's pants. Rosemarie was very embarrassed, and the *Star Revue* editor apologized to Elvis on her behalf. It is not clear if Elvis knew that Rosemarie had polio, but he smiled and acted like the accident did not bother him.

Elvis signed his autograph to Rosemarie on a picture of him in his white ruffled shirt, the same picture that now hangs prominently in the Graceland foyer. Soon, their exclusive visit with The King of Rock and Roll was over, so Elvis kissed each of them on the cheek and wished them good-bye.

Several photos were taken that day of the meeting, and it was a wonderful memory for Rosemarie, who wrote about her experience years later. Considering the odds of all the girls in Germany who wanted to meet Elvis, Rosemarie was lucky enough to be one of the few to get a private date with him.

Meanwhile, there were plenty of other girls in Germany trying to get their own date with The King of Rock and Roll. There are rumors and stories that have surfaced over the years of several other women that Elvis dated while he was in Germany, although the stories are sometimes questionable.

One German girl who says she dated Elvis was 16-year-old Roswitha Klaus. She lived near Bad Nauheim and claims she was introduced to Elvis one day in December 1958 by Elisabeth. She says she dated Elvis until he returned to the U.S. 14 months later. She said they often went for walks late at night to avoid being seen by the fans.

"He was so sensitive and romantic and such a good kisser," recalled Roswitha. "I would put on makeup for him – although he didn't really like that. He preferred natural, shy girls."

Roswitha's story seems believable due to the existence of a few photos taken of her with Elvis. During the summer of 1959, she was photographed with Elvis relaxing and frolicking on the grass where Presley was playing football with his friends. In one of the photos, Elvis is sitting on top of her as she lay on the grass. He is holding her hands up and they are both smiling flirtatiously at each other. It just may be the most playful photo of Elvis ever taken.

"Elvis sang some songs in German, but he couldn't speak the language," explained Roswitha. "And I only had nine weeks of English lessons at school. So we communicated with hands and feet… He would sit on the edge of the bed, play his guitar and sing 'Love Me Tender' just for me."

While some of Presley's dates kept their personal lives private, others were – and still are – willing to kiss and tell. The most recent past love of Elvis to write a memoir is Heli von Westrem (formerly Heli Priemel). In 2020, von Westrem published a book (in German) about her relationship with Elvis in Germany from late May 1959 through March 1960. The story of their first meeting is suspected to be the motivation for an embellished story that made it into *BRAVO* later that year.

One afternoon, right before her 16th birthday, Heli and her older sister, Isa-Vera, drove to Elvis house in Bad Nauheim from their home in Frankfurt. When they pulled up in their blue Opel Kapitan with whitewall tires, of course, Elvis took notice since he was a fan of this German brand of cars. According to Heli, all of a sudden, Presley's friend, Cliff Gleaves, and then Elvis jumped into the car with the girls.

Isa-Vera was in the driver's seat, but Heli had stepped out of the car to try to see Elvis. That allowed Cliff Gleaves to get in the front passenger seat. Elvis then came over and got in the back seat pulling Heli in with him.

"'Let's go!' Elvis shouted, in a tone that seemed to mean: 'Now get out of here quickly so that the fans don't follow us'," Heli recounted.

What seemed like an exciting car ride somehow turned into a story of "Kidnapping." Reporter Thomas Beyl wrote a series of articles for *BRAVO* that were published from late 1959 to early 1960. One of the articles was promoted with the headline "Elvis Presley was kidnapped!" on the December 26, 1959 cover.

The story of Elvis riding in the Opel Kapitan got turned around saying that the girls approached Elvis and asked him to sign some autographs so they could prove to their friends on a bet that they met him. They suggested he get in the car and sit down to be more comfortable, and then the girl in the driver's seat stepped on the accelerator and took off without warning Elvis in advance.

The girls were described as being very pretty and from Frankfurt, which corresponds with Heli and her sister. Heli had started modeling and was very attractive. In the article, Elvis was quoted as saying that the girls were driving an Opel Kapitan, which was also true. But that's where the similarity stops.

In the article, Elvis claims that he got mad at the girls, but was not frightened by them. He ordered them to stop so he could get out of the car and start walking home. The article says that Presley's bodyguard, Lamar, who was startled by this event as he watched it unfold, did not even attempt to try to follow them by car, which seems unlikely if Elvis had really been kidnapped.

Thomas Beyl revealed years later that *BRAVO* took his original article and edited and "embellished" it in order to split it up into a multi-part series. He does not mention any kidnapping years later, and even Heli briefly mentions the kidnapping story in her book as "delicious" implying it was a fun adaptation of what really happened.

What seems more likely is Heli's version of the story. Elvis, Cliff, Heli and her sister drove up to the top of Johannisberg Mountain, a popular hangout for tourists and residents alike. A popular café and hotel sat at the top of a hill providing a beautiful panoramic view of Bad Nauheim and the surrounding Wetterau region (named for the Wetter river in the state of Hesse, Germany). Elvis was known to have visited the café on occasion.

Their little adventure seemed to be the furthest thing from a kidnapping. Cliff and Elvis bought the girls ice cream, and they enjoyed the scenery from the top of the mountain. Although as it got darker, Heli described Elvis as getting spooked for a moment thinking he would be attacked by people lurking in the dark. However, his attention quickly shifted to Heli and they started kissing in the back seat of the car. This was the start of their romance.

"Elvis and I… kissed and forgot everything around us," Heli recalled. "It was heaven!"

A few weeks later, after Elvis returned from his first Paris trip, Heli claims she spent time alone with Elvis for the first time, and after that she was referred to as Elvis' "girlfriend" to his friends. Elvis called her "the girl with the beautiful legs" or just "Legs" for short.

Meanwhile, in early May 1959, Presley's bodyguard and friend, Red West left Germany to return to the U.S. Red had a reputation of getting into fist fights, especially when he drank at the nearby Beck's bar. While it is uncertain if Elvis and Vernon asked him to leave due to his combative behavior, Red had every reason to be frustrated during his time in Germany. As Lamar explained, he and Red were both treated poorly by Vernon. They got into shouting matches with him, fueled by the fact that he would not pay them hardly any money.

As a result, Elvis asked Cliff Gleaves to come and take Red's place. He arrived in Germany in late May/early June 1959. Cliff was not your typical Presley bodyguard. A former DJ and aspiring comedian and entertainer, Gleaves was extremely handsome and very independent. While in Germany, Gleaves spent just as much time with other friends exploring Europe, than he did with Elvis. In fact, when he arrived in Germany on Elvis' dime, he initially only stayed in Bad Nauheim for two weeks. In mid-June, he borrowed Presley's Volkswagen and left for a month. Gleaves went to hang out with his new friend, airman Currie Grant, who ran a weekly variety show for the Air Force's Eagle Club in Wiesbaden.

Heli, who spoke English, would spend many nights at Presley's house with Elvis and his friends as he would sing for them. Cliff, Currie and Vernon would take turns driving her from Frankfurt to Bad Nauheim so she could see Elvis. She enjoyed the summer months occupying most of Elvis' attention, but that would soon change.

While the relationship drama between Elvis and girls like Margit Buergin, Vera Tschechowa and Jane Wilbanks made his personal life eventful during the first half of his stay in Germany, things were going to heat up even more in the remaining months.

.

19

BONJOUR, MONSIEUR PRESLEY

On June 1, 1959, Elvis was promoted to Specialist 4th Class. The army explained that Presley was promoted as soon as he became eligible for having served the required time in grade "because of his excellent service record." However, soon after hearing this good news, Elvis came down with tonsilitis and was admitted to the 97th General Hospital in Frankfurt. Elvis suffered an abscessed tonsil and had a high fever of 102 degrees. He was treated in the hospital from June 3 to June 9.

Press reports started circulating as soon as June 4 in the U.S. that Elvis had been hospitalized. This news caused concern among his fans. Presley was asked in an interview later that month if he would have his tonsils removed and he replied, "Not unless it's absolutely necessary."

At the same time, Elvis was itching to go to Paris. He told a reporter in March that he would go if he got the chance. Just four days after being released from the hospital, Elvis got his wish. On June 12, 1959, Elvis and his entourage began their two-week furlough first with a short trip to Munich and then on to Paris. Since Cliff Gleaves decided to go hang out with Currie Grant, he did not go on the trip. Instead, Elvis invited Rex Mansfield and Charlie Hodge to accompany him and Lamar.

Noticeably absent was Presley's father. While Elvis embarked on a few weeks of excitement and adventure in Europe, Vernon headed back to the States, arriving June 24 after an eight-day ship ride, in pursuit of Dee Stanley. He had been having a secret affair with the married mother-of-three for several months now behind her husband's back. The relationship was quite scandalous to those that found out about it in Bad Nauheim. As a result, Dee decided to take her three sons, Billy, Ricky and David, back to their hometown in Virginia to "get away and think". During his return visit, Vernon attended Colonel Parker's 50th birthday party on June 26 in Madison, Tennessee.

Meanwhile, Elvis and his friends traveled by train from Frankfurt to Munich and arrived on a Friday night. They stayed in rooms 136 and 137 at the Hotel Bayrischer Hof for three days spending each night at the Moulin Rouge. Elvis wanted to show his friends, Charlie and Rex, what it was like at this nighttime cabaret and strip club he had frequented in March "for old times sake."

Elvis and his friends would sit in the balcony where they could look down onto the stage. Elvis had his own booth and was accompanied by two or three dancers at a time. Rex, Charlie and Lamar also had their own booths. One night, the dancer sitting with Rex Mansfield had an angry boyfriend who came over and dragged his girlfriend away. Feeling a responsibility to defend her honor, Rex followed the guy and ended up getting in an altercation with him. When Elvis saw what was happening, he came over to help Rex beat the guy up.

In a prelude to his role as a boxer in *Kid Galahad*, Elvis seemed to revel in the fight, whispering "Kill the bastard" to Mansfield, even though he was acting like he was trying to break it up. As Elvis held the man's arms back, Rex was able to get in a strong blow which knocked the guy unconscious. When the club's manager came over, Elvis gave an "Oscar-worthy" apology, according to Rex. As a result, the unconscious man was taken out of the club, and his girlfriend was subsequently fired. Elvis would re-tell the story about the fight over and over again to his friends, making "Rexadus" feel like a hero.

The next night at the Moulin Rouge, a stripper named Marianne did a special erotic dance routine for Elvis onstage where the only thing she wore was a Presley record with his picture on it covering her crotch. Elvis missed the routine because he was trying to break up a disturbance between his bodyguards and a photographer trying to get a picture of Elvis. Later, Marianne and two other strippers joined Presley at his table in the balcony. The Associated Press reported that "Elvis had lots of fun and let the champagne corks pop" (even though Elvis did not drink alcohol).

Unlike his previous trip to Munich in March, for the most part, Elvis was able to maintain his privacy during this trip. Most likely, Presley's incognito status was due to the fact that Vera Tschechowa and her mother were out of the picture. Elvis did not contact them this time. When telephoned by the press if they would be seeing Elvis during his trip, Vera immediately passed the phone to her mother.

"Elvis is always welcome to visit," Ada replied, "but I have asked him to leave his bodyguards at home. I do not like those 'hulks'."

The day he left Munich, on June 15, Elvis did a brief interview in his hotel with German journalist Hannelore Krab. The two were photographed in front of the hotel. She asked Elvis why he would not perform in concert in Germany.

"I was sent over here by the army as a soldier, and it would not be fair to the other boys in the army if I were traveling around and singing," Presley replied. "I cannot be treated any different from the other boys. I am very sorry that I am not over here as an entertainer, as a singer. But maybe, I hope, when I'm out of the army someday I can come back to Europe on a tour and I will travel around as an entertainer."

Never having been to Paris before, Elvis welcomed Colonel Parker's help in arranging for him to have his own personal tour guides. That came in the form of Freddy Bienstock, manager at Hill and Range music publishing who was in charge of finding new songs for Elvis, and his cousin, Jean Aberbach, one of the owners of Hill and Range. Jean was living in London at the time. He spoke fluent French and would serve well as a translator for Elvis. Jean had also lived in Paris for several years prior. At The Colonel's request, Bienstock and Aberbach, who brought along Hill and Range attorney, Ben Starr, flew over to Paris specifically to set up a press conference and to keep an eye on Elvis making sure he stayed out of trouble.

Elvis and his friends arrived in Paris by train early in the morning while it was still dark outside on Tuesday, June 16. When Freddy and Jean greeted them, they urged Elvis to go see the sun rise. Elvis agreed and the group drove out to the countryside on the edge of Paris to await this beautiful act of nature.

As Charlie Hodge vividly described, "the first glow of sunlight splashed pale yellow gold over the fantastic white dome of the Sacre Coeur Church. The Seine River turned into a winding rope of light. Sunlight turned the stained glass in Notre Dame Cathedral into a flickering fire of a thousand colors."

Needless to say, Elvis and the boys were impressed. Charlie said that Elvis never forgot that moment, often recalling: "On a French hillside at dawn – what a way to see the city of Paris for the first time."

After checking into the luxurious Prince de Galles Hotel, just two blocks from the Arc de Triomphe, Elvis and his entourage took a stroll on the Champs-Élysées, one of the world's most famous avenues. Accompanied by Freddy and Jean, Elvis, who was dressed in uniform, along with Charlie, Rex and Lamar were photographed walking through the streets of Paris. While on leave, Presley was not required to dress in uniform, but he personally preferred to do so. This made Elvis stand out even more, since his fellow G.I.s, Rex and Charlie, were dressed in civilian clothes.

Photographers shot several rolls of film that day capturing Presley's stroll through the "City of Lights" as he peered in the window of a high-end men's clothing store and walked by local movie cinemas. Although the entourage was told that Elvis would not be bothered by people in Paris, a large crowd started to congregate around The King of Rock and Roll.

Elvis was mobbed at the Fouquet's outdoor café where they sat down for a quick refreshment. Photos were taken as a young shoeshine boy proceeded to shine Presley's boots. Elvis happily complied to sign autographs when asked. However, as the crowd became larger and larger, they realized that Elvis had to find a way to escape. According to Charlie Hodge, they walked into a movie theater and quickly exited through the back door.

Jean and Freddy had set up sightseeing tours for Elvis, but he didn't seem all that interested: "We only went sightseeing once," Bienstock recalled. "He wanted to see the Eiffel Tower, and he took one look at it and said, 'Well, that's it, let's move on.' He didn't want to go to the Louvre, and he had no feeling for museums at all."

It soon became evident that Elvis was more interested in going to the nightclubs than being a tourist. So much for keeping Elvis out of trouble! The first night they went out, Elvis stayed dressed in his uniform. He gave each of the guys $100 bills.

"You guys just use this for tips," he said. "I'll pay the bill... and tip them heavy. We want to look good."

According to Mansfield, their nightly routine consisted of first going to see the early shows at nightclubs like the Folies Bergère, Moulin Rouge, Le Carrousel and Le Café de Paris, before catching the late show at the

Lido. The first night, Mr. Aberbach was photographed with a uniformed Elvis as he autographed playbills outside the Folies Bergère.

The next day on June 17, 1959, French newspapers ran articles with photographs of Elvis in uniform walking around the Champs-Élysées with headlines like "Le Sergeant Presley en permission de détente a Paris," meaning "Sergeant Presley on leave to relax in Paris." Notably, they mistakenly labeled Elvis as a sergeant, although he was not a sergeant at this time.

On the afternoon of June 17 at 4:30 p.m., Elvis held a press conference in one of the meeting rooms of the hotel. This was quite memorable for the French press since it would be the one and only time they had direct contact with the American superstar. There were also non-French outlets in attendance including the American Forces Network (AFN), and some pretty girls were believed to have snuck in amongst the reporters. Presley quickly relaxed as he answered reporters' questions asked in English, or translated from French by Mr. Aberbach.

"Elvis was so much like one of the guys when he was offstage, but in the spotlight he was transformed," described Rex Mansfield. "He did an extraordinary job of interacting with the press and was the consummate professional."

When asked what he thought of Paris, Elvis replied: "Ah! Paris, what a city - all those cafes on the sidewalk and women who don't seem in a hurry...What do I want to do in Paris? Lose myself in the crowd and have fun like a kid..."

As one French reporter described, Elvis looked so dapper in his "strict black suit, white shirt with iced collar, and pearl gray tie." He was also wearing a monogrammed "E" handkerchief in his lapel. Quite a surprise when compared to the image of Elvis as a rebellious rock and roll star. The fashion of Paris had a long-lasting effect on Elvis, and his more sophisticated look was a hint of things to come.

"Tight, continental slacks, sweaters that stressed the breadth of the shoulders, and medium-length hair controlled by hairsprays would affect his sense of style," observed authors Brown and Broeske. "Presley came home [from Europe] with suitcases of continental clothes."

After the press conference was over, Elvis continued talking to reporters informally on the adjoining patio in the courtyard located in the middle of hotel. Then, the crowd of reporters followed Elvis outside. On the sidewalk in front of the hotel, Elvis was photographed kissing the hand of a young woman. He then got into his rented white Cadillac parked in front of the hotel to take a drive around Paris.

Later that night, Elvis and his entourage went to the Lido cabaret and burlesque nightclub for the first time and watched the show "Avec Plaisir!" which means "With Pleasure." The revue featured a lineup of dancers called The Bluebell Girls, known for their statuesque height averaging 5'11", who would support the main performers. This special dance troupe at the Lido featured the tallest and most beautiful dancers who seemed to tower over the other performers with their glitzy costumes and high heels. As a result, The Bluebell Girls dance troupe became the most popular attraction at the Lido shows.

"The Lido girls fell in love with Elvis," explained Charlie Hodge. "They always let Elvis go backstage at the Lido. The show girls would gang around him. He'd invite them all to come along with us when we left after the last show."

The Bluebell Girls sometimes appeared topless and/or nude during the show. Many were young girls from England. Some were classical dancers who were too tall to be professional ballerinas. Charlie Hodge described a performance where The Bluebell Girls portrayed mannequins that "framed the scenes on stage like Greek sculptures. Beautiful to behold. They looked like fine paintings borrowed from a big museum miraculously brought to life. We didn't think they were vulgar in any way."

"We were permitted to go backstage every night after the show," Rex Mansfield described. "There, the show girls all roamed about naked, without batting an eyelash. I just about fainted at this sight."

The next day on June 18, 1959, the largest daily newspaper in France, France-soir, published a front-page story with photos of Elvis at the Lido. The headline (translated) read: "Elvis Presley, the highest paid US singer in the world, wanted to go unnoticed in Paris." The news that Elvis was visiting Paris also made it to American readers. The Associate Press reported on June 19 that "Paris Bubbles Over Presley."

Among all the girls to choose from at the Lido, there were a few that Elvis was especially fond of. Charlie Hodge said that Elvis dated one of the Bluebell dancers from England, named Della, whose twin sister was also in the show. Elvis was also interested in a red-headed American ice skater from the show, Nancy Parker, British dancer Jane Clarke, and also one of the Kessler twin sisters. Alice and Ellen Kessler were favorites in the show and were from Nerchau, Germany.

After the show was over at The Lido club, Elvis and his friends would go to a small club called Le Bantu, or The 4 o'Clock Club, which was the hangout for show business people in Paris. The club did not open until 4 am.

"We usually arrived [at Le Bantu] around 4:30 a.m. with our string of girls from the Lido," recalled Rex Mansfield. "Elvis always picked out two of the best-looking ones and we were left with the rest. They were all gorgeous to us. Around 9 a.m., we left with several of The Bluebell Girls in tow, who accompanied us back to our hotel."

Presley's promiscuity was at full throttle during his time in Europe. As Lamar Fike described: "Elvis had no compunction about that kind of stuff. To him, it was just banging. He had absolutely no guilt and no trouble balancing his behavior with his religious beliefs."

As Freddy Bienstock described: "You wouldn't believe it. He [Elvis] was there for 10 days and he made it with 22 of the 24 girls. (laughs) It was unbelievable. There was one coming in the front and one leaving in the back. The overflow was too hard to handle. (laughs)"

Elvis felt like he was in Las Vegas again as he mingled with the entertainers and showgirls at the different Paris nightclubs. One night when Elvis was at the Moulin Rouge, he was summoned backstage by the star of the show. African-American singer Nancy Holloway, who was performing there, wrote Presley a note which read: "Elvis, could you do me one last big favor and come backstage immediately after the finale?" Elvis wrote back: "I will be at the entrance to the backstage as you asked. E.P."

Nancy was interested in getting some pictures with Elvis that night. The Moulin Rouge photographer took many photos of Elvis with Nancy and others, including French actor André Pousse, and another performer on the bill, Italian entertainer, Torrebruno. Nancy and Elvis became friends and he would often go see her perform at the Mars Club, a jazz club she would perform at after-hours.

"He's someone I'll always love, not only for the character he was, but also for the man I knew," Holloway reminisced years later. "I didn't know Elvis, the showman. When he was here, he was a man like everyone else, very relaxed… At the time I used to sing 'Fever' quite often and Elvis told me: 'Why, I forgot that… When I come home, I'm going to record it.' And he recorded it."

At the Lido, Elvis was also photographed with comedian George Bernard, who had a long-running show at the club. Several months later, Bernard revealed details about the night that Elvis sang at the Lido club in secret. After the show was over one night, Bernard was coming out of his dressing room and he heard someone playing the piano and singing so quietly. Bernard never expected it to be Elvis!

Bernard then saw Elvis playing the piano surrounded by the staff of the Lido Club including waiters, cleaners, busboys and security personnel. They were getting a free concert by Elvis. Bernard was surprised that Presley was singing songs like a soft bluesy number called "Willow Weep for Me." This song was considered a jazz standard and had been recorded by singers like Billie Holiday and Frank Sinatra.

"It wasn't the Elvis we know on records," Bernard described. "This was a suave, sophisticated songster at the piano, making magic at the keyboard, and singing in a soft, well-modulated, superbly controlled voice. Elvis sang for about a half an hour, a dreamy, contented expression on his face. He was enjoying himself."

When asked why he decided to perform impromptu that night, Elvis replied: "I had the urge. I play quite a bit back in my home in Germany, singing at the piano. Guess being in Paris I missed my piano and when I saw that one on the stage there I couldn't resist it."

Surprisingly, the U.P.I. wire service had distributed a short article in the States from June 20, 1959 immediately after the private show. Elvis was quoted as saying that he was "hauled up on the stage" at the Lido and that he experienced stage fright having been away from performing for so long. The details of the performance were not made clear in the article, but it seems like Elvis may have intentionally played down the fact that he volunteered to perform, especially since any public performance while he was in the army was a no-no in Colonel Parker's eyes.

George Bernard questioned Elvis as to why he performed rock and roll professionally since he could sing so well as a crooner, as evident by his private Lido concert. Elvis replied: "I have a lot of fans who like me rocking. I like rocking, too. So we have a good time. When they want me singing softer ballads – I'm ready. Till then, I go on rocking."

Here was tangible proof of how Elvis' true musical passions were not necessarily linked with his commercial success. The more free time Presley had in the army, the more his musical expressions shifted to the styles he truly enjoyed singing. As early as 1956, Elvis was giving hints of which styles of music he preferred. In a June 1956 interview, Elvis said his favorite song of his own up to that point was not his big hit "Heartbreak Hotel" – the song that would inspire so many future musicians to sing rock and roll - but rather the ballad "I Was The One."

While John Lennon unfairly stated years later that "Elvis died when he went into the army," what he meant was that the "rock and roll" Elvis had disappeared. It wasn't that the army changed Elvis, it was that The King of Rock and Roll had the courage to finally shift closer to the music that he enjoyed performing the most.

"Elvis loved opera, and he especially liked Mario Lanza," Marty Lacker explained. "He loved the power of the big voices. And he loved big orchestras. He liked real dramatic things. He'd see these maestros conducting, and he would get up and imitate them, standing in front of the television."

Since being in Germany, Elvis had been practicing almost nightly on his singing, especially when Charlie Hodge would come over to his home in Bad Nauheim. Elvis wanted to expand his vocal range, and with Charlie's help, he started singing more from his diaphragm instead of his throat.

Presley's singing bond with Hodge went full force in a taxi one night in Paris as they were driving near the Eiffel Tower. As they were on their way to the Lido club driving on the Champs-Élysées, Elvis, Charlie and Rex started singing and harmonizing their favorite songs like "I'll Be Home Again" and various spirituals. Elvis was enjoying it so much that he told the driver to keep turning around: "One more time," Elvis said. "Up to the Arch [Arc de Triomphe] and back."

It was a trip that Elvis did not want to end – so much so that on June 26 he canceled the group's train reservations and rented a limo with a driver to take them back to Friedberg. That way they could stay an extra night and still make it back to their base in time before midnight on June 27. The Paris trip cost Elvis $12,800 back in 1959, which would be approximately $115,000 in today's dollars. But they all agreed it was worth every cent!

In a letter dated July 1, 1959, Lamar wrote a letter on behalf of Elvis thanking Jean Aberbach for his help during their trip: "I don't know what we would have done without you on that trip, because of the press, and all the reporters," Lamar wrote. "You were absolutely marvelous in the way that you handled them… thank you from the bottom of our hearts, for making everything go right. This is something that Elvis or myself will never forget."

Unfortunately for Elvis, one thing did not go right during his trip. His quest to meet Brigitte Bardot went unfulfilled. When Presley was asked about her at the Paris press conference, he declared: "Brigitte Bardot? She's the eighth wonder of the world!" However, Elvis tried calling her during his trip but never got a response. That would be understandable since, to many people's surprise, an already pregnant Bardot had just married French actor, Jacques Charrier, on June 18, just a few days after Elvis had arrived in Paris.

One aspect that made the Paris trip unforgettable were the encounters Elvis and the guys had with transgender women at several of the Paris nightclubs. In fact, the Carousel club was famous for a cabaret show by the transgender performer, Coccinelle. It was hard for Elvis and his friends to decipher which good-looking women were genetically men underneath. Lamar was fooled when he asked Elvis to set him up with a particular showgirl. She came out to meet Lamar, but when things got intimate, he was horrified to learn that the "she" was physically a "he." Elvis got a big kick out of it since someone told him ahead of time. But from that point on, Elvis and Lamar were always suspicious of any new girls they would meet in Paris nightclubs.

"When he came back, [Elvis] had a program from the Carousel club which he was showing to the guys in the barracks," recalled Presley's army buddy, Pat Conway. "Those who saw the pictures were making comments like; 'Wow, she is a really good-looking gal. She's a knockout!' After everyone kept going on like that, he lowered the boom on them: 'Sorry, but these are all guys.' That was kind of a good trick he laid on everybody."

The exciting time Elvis had in Paris in June prompted him to go back again for a short weekend trip in July 1959. Elvis, Charlie and Lamar were accompanied not by Rex this time, but by Corporal Pat Conway who was in the same platoon as Elvis in Friedberg. While there was not much fanfare on this trip since it was so short, Conway confirmed that they went to the Lido, the Carousel club and Le Bantu. But it wasn't just the nightlife that Elvis enjoyed.

"There was another reason Elvis liked Paris," Lamar Fike explained. "He'd get in a funk and worry about whether he was still hot..." All the crowds he attracted and all the attention he got "made him feel like he was still on top." Or as Elvis told a reporter: "It [Paris] reminds me so much of the life I used to live before I went into the service."

20

A PRINCE MEETS THE KING

Coming up on August 14, 1959, Elvis was facing the one-year anniversary of his mother's untimely death. Even though for the past year he had been busy fulfilling his army duties and exploring the nightlife of Munich and Paris with his friends, Elvis still had a hard time processing his grief.

Elvis sought comfort and consultation with an Army Chaplain in his brigade in Germany. He would often confide in Monsignor Thaddeus F. Malanowski about the great loss of his mother. Although the conversational details between a person and his clergy are kept confidential, The Monsignor said this about his relationship with Presley: "Elvis would occasionally visit with me… He showed me some photos of his mother and wondered if I knew of a particular Catholic civilian priest in Memphis, Tennessee. I said I didn't, and he told me that this priest, a chaplain at the hospital where his mom had died, had visited her almost daily."

"I've talked to my chaplain lots of times, about big things and little things, and I expect to keep up this practice," Elvis said after he got out of the army in 1960. "Right after my mother died, I don't know what I would have done if my chaplain hadn't helped me."

Since Vernon Presley, who was already seriously involved with another woman, would not return to Germany until later that month, Elvis had no one to share in the grief he was still feeling for his mother. It was hard for Elvis to see his father move on so quickly after his mother's death, and neither he nor his grandmother cared for Dee Stanley.

"That woman is making a fool out of my daddy," Elvis told his Memphis girlfriend, Anita Wood. "She really knows how to work him."

Fate stepped in with a much-needed distraction for Elvis as he met with Hal Wallis, producer for his upcoming movie which would eventually be named *G.I. Blues*. Wallis visited Presley in Bad Nauheim to discuss the movie and see how his most valuable actor under contract was doing. Filming of background footage and location shots for *G.I. Blues* began on Monday, August 17.

The filming lasted for three weeks and a body-double was used for Elvis. Private First Class T.W. Creel, a native of Mississippi, was chosen because, as Wallis stated: "He'll look like Elvis from a distance. He has the same characteristic walk and mannerisms as Presley... in other respects he's a dead ringer for Elvis." Creel would continue to play Presley's double in two more movies including *Girls! Girls! Girls!* and *Fun in Acapulco*.

It was reported that background scene shots of Presley's unit were being made with the army's cooperation, and about 100 of the 3rd Armored Division's soldiers were working as extras in the film. However, no scenes in Germany were shot with Elvis. Due to Colonel Parker's insistence, Presley would not be filmed for *G.I. Blues* until the following year in 1960 in Hollywood after he left the army.

Instead, Elvis was enjoying a secret getaway at a nearby camping grounds and swimming lake called Lake Gedern, which was about 45 minutes northeast of Ray Barracks. Presley wanted a change of scenery and an escape from public scrutiny. Under the guise that he could continue his duties, like keeping up the maintenance of his battalion jeep, Elvis found a way to spend time at this recreation area.

It was reported that Presley rented a room at the Finger Inn at Lake Gedern for one to two weeks. Elvis enjoyed himself riding his bike around the lake and taking short drives in a Messerschmitt bubble car. Elvis was photographed several times at Lake Gedern from late August through early September 1959.

However, Elvis ended up exchanging one form of attention from soldiers at the barracks to another form of attention from all the vacationers at the lake. There are many photos of fans in their bathing suits posing with Elvis at Lake Gedern (or *Gederner See* in German), but he is always pictured wearing his army uniform. That is because he only visited the lake during the daytime while he was on duty.

It was an exciting surprise for the many fans that got to meet Presley by chance at the lake. In recognition, there is now a memorial stone recognizing Presley's visits to Lake Gedern, which reads: "In memory of

Elvis A. Presley who liked to linger at Lake Gerden during his military service in 1959."

A 15-year-old boy named Peter Weidemann who lived in the town of Usingen recalled seeing Elvis at a different swimming lake on August 14, 1959, the one-year anniversary of his mother's passing. This four-acre manmade lake called the Hattsteinweiher was a magnet for sunbathers and campers, and only a 30-minute ride from Friedberg. Many congregated at Uncle Gustav's Hut, an outdoor venue serving refreshments. That Friday, Elvis was sitting at one of the tables with two army companions, including Sgt. Billy Wilson, who had taken Sgt. Ira Jones' place.

As teenager Peter headed to the lake for an afternoon of fun, he saw his friend Hermann Wöhlermann who alerted him that Elvis had been spotted at the lake. Peter rode home on his friend's bike to retrieve his camera. Both fans of The King of Rock and Roll, Weidemann and his friend made it back to the lake with a camera and transistor radio in hand and approached Presley's table.

Luckily for Peter and his friends, not many people recognized Elvis, who was dressed in his army fatigues. They asked Elvis if they could sit at the table with him and he agreed. Several young girls also approached the table to ask Elvis for autographs. Elvis treated them and many others to free refreshments, like his favorite drink Pepsi-Cola.

Peter was impressed with how patient Elvis was in signing all the autographs, but he was surprised by Presley's quiet mood. "I noticed that he was not happy," Peter recalled years later, which prompted him to ask Elvis to take a walk around the lake with his friends as they listened to his portable radio. There are photos of Elvis with Peter and his friends, as well as Elvis holding Peter's radio. Elvis started to smile in those photos where he's wearing sunglasses, signifying that this sincere group of teenagers were able to distract him for a while from his depressed mood. They even got a photo with Elvis in front of his Cadillac before he left.

Presley returned to Hattsteinweiher a second time and took an intriguing photo. Elvis in uniform is posing with a few older women, but he supported himself by hanging his arms on their shoulders so his legs could float in the air. Weidemann believes that Elvis was in such a playful mood because one of the women held a strong resemblance to his mother, Gladys. Mrs. Hoffman was the midwife for Usingen and had short, dark wavy hair and a round face like Mrs. Presley.

As Weidemann realized years later, Hattsteinweiher and Lake Gedern must have reminded Elvis of his childhood days spent by the lake in Tupelo, Mississippi where he grew up. The scenery hopefully gave the 24-year-old Elvis some refuge from his grief and feeling homesick.

Meanwhile, another distraction for Elvis in dealing with his sorrow was a surprise phone call he received in mid-August 1959. One of the princes of Saudi Arabia was in town and wanted to meet The King of Rock and Roll. Elvis welcomed the request and invited Prince Abdullah, the thirteenth son of Ibn Saud, the King of Saudi Arabia, to come to his home at 14 Goethestrasse on Saturday afternoon, August 22, 1959.

The Presley family had shown traditional southern hospitality by welcoming various visitors to stay at their house in Bad Nauheim, including journalist Thomas Beyl. A foreign correspondent for *BRAVO* who had known Elvis since 1956, Beyl just happened to be staying at the house when Prince Abdullah visited Elvis. He witnessed the entire meeting between Presley and the Prince, who was a big Elvis fan.

It was a surprise that the Prince, who would hold the title of Mayor of Mecca starting in 1961, would want the meeting. In the Muslim world, rock and roll was considered the devil's work. However, when the Prince came to visit The King of Rock and Roll, he treated Elvis like royalty. The Prince entered the house with two servants, who presented Elvis with a set of gifts.

Presley received a royal arabic black kaftan, with golden strands on the arms, as well as a traditional headscarf, just like what the Prince was wearing. As Beyl described, this was "not the robe of the common people, but the rank of a prince was offered to Elvis." In addition, Elvis was given a tea service including a tray decorated in the theme of "1001 Nights" along with cups and glasses bearing the state coat of arms of Saudi Arabia.

Embarrassed that he had no gifts to offer, Elvis gave an autographed picture of himself to the Prince, who seemed very appreciative. For the next hour, The King and The Prince sat in the living room to chat. The Presley entourage, which included Vernon, Lamar, Cliff and Elisabeth, learned that the Prince had been studying in London and was very open to Western culture.

Elvis was beyond excited about the gifts he received. He put the Arabic robe on and modeled the headscarf for his friends. There are several photos of Elvis wearing the robe and headscarf sometimes with sunglasses. One includes Elvis posing with his father who is wearing a white robe. He even sent one of the photos to Anita Wood where he drew in a mustache and goatee on his face to look similar to the Prince. He signed the photo: "Love you always, from 'The Thing'."

With Presley's enthusiasm for the Arabian clothes, journalist Thomas Beyl thought Presley may wear the clothes later on when he went out for his nightly autograph session in front of the house from 7:30 to 8:00 p.m. However, Elvis chose not to.

Just six years later, Elvis would appear in an Arabian-themed film called *Harum Scarum*. Little did his fans know that not only was Presley used to wearing the traditional Arabian headscarf, but also welcomed it, thanks to the meeting with the Prince in Bad Nauheim in 1959. This "secret" meeting between the reigning King of Rock and Roll and a future King of Saudi Arabia never made it into the papers.

Notably, Prince Abdullah, who was one of 45 sons of King Ibn Saud, went on to become the King of Saudi Arabia from 2005 to his death in 2015. A more moderate King, he gave women the right to vote for municipal councils and implemented a government scholarship program for young men and women to study in universities around the world.

21

MEETING AN ANGEL

Just a few weeks after Presley's escape to the nearby lakes, he would get the ultimate distraction he needed to take his mind off of his mother's death. On a Sunday night in the fall of 1959, Elvis was introduced to an enchanting young girl named Priscilla Beaulieu (pronounced "bowl-yo"). While the story of how Priscilla got to meet Elvis may appear simple and romantic, it was actually a bit complicated.

Fate was on 14-year-old Priscilla's side as she arrived in Germany on August 15, 1959 with her family. Her stepfather, Captain Paul Beaulieu, had been transferred from Bergstrom Air Force Base in Austin, Texas to Wiesbaden, Germany, which was an hour from Bad Nauheim. Priscilla was sad to leave her friends in Texas, but was happy to know that she would be living in the vicinity of Elvis Presley, and told a friend that she would meet Elvis.

"Small and petite, with long brown hair, blue eyes, and an upturned nose, I was always stared at by the other students," Priscilla recalled in her 1985 memoir, *Elvis and Me.* "People always said I was the prettiest girl in school, but I never felt that way." In fact, Priscilla was named "Best Looking Senior" in her 12th grade high school yearbook.

Priscilla may have been a shy 14-year-old girl, but she was also confident and determined. Born May 24, 1945, she was a classic Gemini exhibiting dual natures – on one side, timid and reserved, and on the other, bold and assertive. As a young girl, Priscilla said she had a strong feeling that whatever she was going to do in life, "it was chosen for me. And it was going to create a very big effect."

While it is common knowledge that Currie Grant was the one to bring Priscilla over to Presley's house that fateful night, there are conflicting versions of how that came to be. There is a dispute about who brought up the idea to meet Elvis. Grant was in charge of entertainment at the Eagle Club, which was an Air Force community center in Wiesbaden. Every day after school, Priscilla would go to the snack bar there and listen to the jukebox. Grant says Priscilla was there one afternoon and asked him to introduce her to Elvis, while Priscilla says Grant was the one who initially approached her with the idea. However, Grant admits that he did introduce himself to Priscilla several days before they talked about Elvis and invited her to the weekly variety show at the club.

Meanwhile, Presley's friend, Cliff Gleaves, had been spending a great amount of time with Currie Grant and his wife. Lamar Fike had originally met Currie at a benefit show in Giessen in early May 1959 that he attended with Vernon and Elisabeth. Lamar invited Currie and his wife to come meet Elvis in Bad Nauheim. Soon after, The Grants came over on a Sunday afternoon to Bad Nauheim and that is where Elvis and Cliff Gleaves met them. Gleaves was an aspiring comedian who wanted to get booked on the weekly variety show for the Air Force that Grant ran called "Hit Parade."

According to Lamar, Cliff and Currie met Priscilla at a pool in late August. It was actually Cliff who told Elvis about Priscilla and described her to Elvis. Elvis was impressed and said to have Currie bring her over.

Cliff Gleaves' influence on Elvis was not to be underestimated. Cliff "could make Elvis laugh so hard," recalled Anita Wood. "And they used to laugh at such silly things... Elvis and [his cousin] Gene would sit there and talk this weird language, talk to each other so crazy, crazy, crazy, and just die laughing... and Cliff was right there with him."

At this point, Gleaves was strictly a friend and not on Presley's payroll. Gleaves was the one member of Presley's entourage who could compete with Elvis on looks and charm. He was very funny and Elvis really looked up to him. According to Rick Stanley, one of Dee Stanley's sons, Cliff "was like Robin Williams – everyone just sat while he went on a riff. Elvis sat in awe of him... Elvis would fly him in from anywhere just to have him around."

"The meeting with Cliff is what really set the wheels in motion," recalled Lamar. "When Cliff described her to Elvis, I went over to take a look at her. I told Elvis, 'She's as cute as she can be. But God Almighty, she's 14 years old. We'll end up in prison for life'."

The fact that Priscilla was so young did not bother Elvis. In the south, at the time it was not unusual for girls to get married at a young age. As late as 1967, four states still permitted girls at the age of 14 to get married with parental consent including South Carolina and Alabama. As recent as 2018, 16-year-olds could still get married in Tennessee with parental consent.

Ironically, a year before meeting Priscilla, Elvis was asked about the controversy surrounding Jerry Lee Lewis and his recent marriage to his 13-year-old cousin. "He's a great artist," Elvis replied. "I'd rather not talk about his marriage, except that if he really loves her, I guess it's all right."

Currie Grant was an Airman First Class, so it also helped that Captain Beaulieu knew Grant's commanding officer. As a result, when Currie met Priscilla's parents, he assured them that Priscilla would be properly chaperoned by he and his wife when they visited Elvis. (However, the chaperoning did not go as smoothly as planned. Years later, as described in the book *Child Bride*, Priscilla and Currie would have a "he said, she said" debate about what happened on those rides to and from Elvis' house when Grant's wife was not present. In 1998, Priscilla took Currie to court suing him for defamation. The court ruled in her favor.)

The day that Priscilla met Elvis, which most historians agree was Sunday, September 13, 1959, was truly an unforgettable night for both Elvis and Priscilla, as noted by the people who were also there at Presley's house in Bad Nauheim that evening. Wearing a navy and white sailor dress with white socks and shoes, Priscilla had a strong resemblance to Debra Paget, who Elvis had famously been interested in when he was filming *Love Me Tender* with her in 1956.

Priscilla remembered Elvis wearing a red sweater and tan pants. When she walked into the living room, he immediately stood up to meet her. Instantly taken with her beauty, Elvis made small talk with Priscilla. He thought she looked mature enough to be a junior or senior in high school, but Priscilla was only in ninth grade. He then started playing the piano and singing songs like "Great Balls of Fire" imitating Jerry Lee Lewis for her and his friends.

Talking to a girl from the States removed the language barrier Elvis had with many of the German girls he dated. Elvis was curious to find out from Priscilla what music the kids her age were listening to back home. Priscilla assured Elvis they were all listening to his music. Then, Elvis asked Priscilla what kind of music she liked to listen to. She told him:

Mario Lanza, an American opera singer turned film star (who sadly would pass away just a month later at the young age of 38).

"You're kidding. How do you know about Mario Lanza?" Elvis asked. Priscilla said she loved Lanza's album, *The Student Prince*. Elvis was impressed and said that was his favorite.

"For a girl her age, she held her own," recalled Cliff Gleaves.

"Priscilla did have a way about her, when she was around Elvis, that made her seem far older than her 14 years," recalled Charlie Hodge. "She had a kind of poise. An aloofness about her... Elvis told me, over and over, 'Charlie, Priscilla is the most beautiful creature I ever saw'."

During the evening, Priscilla noticed a voluptuous poster of Brigitte Bardot hanging on the wall. This immediately made her feel out of place.

"I'm looking at that picture," Priscilla recalled, "and he looks at it, and I go, 'Did you put that up?' and he goes, 'no.' I go, 'Is that someone you want to see?' He goes, 'Well, you know, she's - you know, she's – she's Brigitte Bardot.' I go, 'I know, but why is it on the door?' He says, 'It's a guy thing. It's a guy thing.'"

How could any woman not be intimidated by a poster of a half-nude young star with a "fulsome body, pouting lips and wild mane of tousled hair"? But later in the evening, Elvis tried to reassure Priscilla: "Baby, you don't have to worry about anything. I'm not looking around for Brigitte Bardot."

That night, Elvis told Rex Mansfield that Priscilla looked like an angel. "And she's young enough that I can train her any way I want," Elvis told him.

"I noticed he had kind of a glazed-over look in his eyes indicating to me that this girl must be something special indeed," described Elisabeth. "She did look like an angel. She reminded me of a painting because she was flawless. She was also very petite, demure and quiet – just what Elvis liked in a woman."

"When Elvis latched onto Priscilla, it wasn't much different than being with Heidi, Gloria, and Frances," said Presley's cousin Billy Smith years later. He was referring to Heidi Heissen, Gloria Mowel and Frances Forbes, the three 14-year-old girls that Elvis used to invite over for private "pajama parties" at his Audobon Drive home and playfully romp around with for hours in his bedroom.

The truth was that Elvis was still seeing other girls when he first met Priscilla. Not only was Elisabeth still living at the house, but Presley kept seeing the 16-year-old German girl, Heli Priemel, who claimed she was at the house the night he met Priscilla. Heli said that on many nights she would be leaving Presley's bedroom as Priscilla arrived. She also claimed that Elvis took her and Priscilla together to the movies a few times.

Imagine how stressful it would be from Priscilla's perspective as a 14-year-old girl dating Elvis to see her competition face-to-face every time she went to visit him. But Priscilla was determined to stay in the running for Elvis' affections.

"Priscilla knew the rules," Currie explained. "She didn't make a fuss about… there being somebody else. Back then she was just happy to go see him."

The competition between Priscilla and Heli continued when Elvis had to be hospitalized again. On October 19, 1959, Presley's army unit went on maneuvers called Operation Big Lift at the military training area in Wildflecken. This mountainous region was the most disliked training area among soldiers due to its high altitude and extreme weather conditions. Elvis was hospitalized starting on October 24, 1959 in Frankfurt for tonsillitis.

Heli describes in her book that Cliff Gleaves called to tell her the news that Elvis was in the hospital. Heli claims that she and Priscilla were driven by Heli's father to the American Military hospital in Frankfurt to visit Elvis. She also says that Elvis had the operation to have his tonsils removed, although all reports, including from Elvis himself, contradict that claim.

However, not only was Elvis hospitalized for five days from October 24 to 29, but he was also ordered to stay home for another three days after his discharge from the hospital. Presley's second bout with tonsillitis made it into papers around the world. After his return from Germany in March 1960, Elvis responded to a question about his tonsils at a press conference at Graceland:

"I had two attacks of tonsillitis when I was there… They don't like to perform surgery of any kind in Europe. They don't like to. If it's an emergency, they will. But I took penicillin and wonder drugs, or whatever they're called."

Meanwhile, Priscilla's version of visiting Elvis in the hospital is quite different, and she never mentions Heli. Priscilla remembers Elvis being hospitalized in January 1960 while he was on maneuvers and says that she was driven to the hospital by Lamar to see him. She claims that Elvis was not sick and that he was faking so that he could escape the harsh conditions out in the field.

"Since the weather was so bad and everyone was so worried about his voice, his answer was tonsillitis," Priscilla revealed. "Already susceptible to catching colds, Elvis learned to dramatize his sickness with a little flick of a match."

However, there are no reports that Elvis was sick or hospitalized during January 1960 when he was on maneuvers. There were several news reports in October 1959 quoting army doctors who confirmed that Presley had a throat infection and his tonsils may need to be removed. Before he went to the hospital, Elvis wrote a letter to Anita from Grafenwoehr complaining that he had tonsilitis and a fever. Elvis returned to Wildflecken on November 2 and remained there for three more weeks to complete maneuvers with his unit.

This is most likely around the time when a 22-year-old Colin Powell, who would go on to become a four-star general and the first African-American Secretary of State, met Elvis. Powell, who was then a First Lieutenant, was stationed in Germany for two years, and he recalled running into the famous rock and roll singer one morning near Giessen. Presley's scout jeep was parked on a narrow road.

"We were in this wooden area north of Frankfurt and I was driving along in my Jeep and somebody noted that, there he was," recalled Powell. "When I got out of my Jeep and walked over to him, he saluted and was very proper, and what struck me was that he looked just like another G.I.... just as dirty and tired as the rest of us from doing his job."

However, Presley's fellow platoon scout, Robert McDaniel, who served with Elvis in the 3rd Armored Division, believes Elvis got special treatment. McDaniel was also a jeep driver, but he pointed out that while his job was to drive a jeep full of soldiers out to scout, Elvis only had to drive the platoon leader. McDaniel seemed to resent the fact that Elvis got to live off-base, even though Presley had every right to since his father and grandmother were dependents. He believed Elvis was treated differently from the rest of the platoon.

"One time, I got a heck of a cold and I went to the infirmary and they gave me a bottle of Aspirin," McDaniel explained. "And Elvis, he got a cold, too. They put him in the hospital."

Another of Presley's fellow soldiers, Private First Class Roger Bevre, roomed with Elvis in Wildflecken. The old barracks they were assigned to sleep in had coal stoves and cold floors. He revealed that Presley bought electric heaters, throw rugs and a lock for the door to the barracks to make their sleeping quarters more comfortable during maneuvers. Sometimes they had to camp outside in sleeping bags. Instead, Elvis preferred to sleep in his jeep with the heater on. According to Bevre, Elvis "caught a cold and had to be air lifted out to a hospital. We heard he was worried about getting laryngitis."

On a few occasions, it appeared that Elvis did get special privileges depending on the circumstances: "I talked with Elvis maybe once a month while he was in Germany and kept up with his life over there," recalled Presley's friend, George Klein. "I learned that as hard as he was trying to be treated like every other soldier, he objected to the custom of having to holler his yes-sir's and no-sir's to his officers: He felt like he was damaging his voice and his livelihood. He was granted permission not to holler."

However, McDaniel admitted that no one seemed to mind that Presley was treated differently. For the most part, "Elvis acted like the rest of the guys."

In the letter Elvis wrote to Anita from Wildflecken before he went to the hospital, Elvis pleaded with Anita not to give up on their relationship:

My Dearest Darling 'Little',

Well here I am. Back out in the field for 30 days again and believe me it's miserable. There is only one consolation, and that is the fact that it [his army service] is almost over... First of all I don't really know how you feel about me now because after all 2 years is a long time in a young girl's life. But I want you to know that in spite of our being apart I have developed a love for you that cannot be equaled or surpassed by anyone... I have been sleeping out on the ground, and I have a fever and tonsillitis again... So darling if you still feel the same and if you love me and me

*alone we will have a great life together even though you hear things and
read things...*

Deep down, Elvis was obviously conflicted. Although he was planning
to return to his relationship with Anita once he left the army, his bright
light in Germany was spending time with Priscilla. The combination of
Priscilla and Minnie Mae had become Elvis' substitute for his mother
Gladys. He'd look to Minnie Mae for motherly advice and he'd look to
Priscilla for the affection and empathy he used to get from his mother. He
even started calling her "Satnin" which was his nickname for his mother.

"She'd soothe him with baby talk, and she'd pet him the way he loved
to be petted," said Lamar Fike.

Priscilla stated in her 1985 book, *Elvis and Me*, that she and Elvis never
had sex until they were married in 1967. She again reiterated that their
relationship remained "chaste" in the *Elvis by The Presleys* book released
in 2005.

"I really felt I got to know who Elvis Presley was during that time,"
Priscilla revealed years later. "Not with ego – not the star that he felt he
should portray. I saw him raw, totally raw, I saw him as he really was after
he lost his mother. We talked so much, he shared his grief with me, he was
very insecure, and he felt very betrayed by his father, that he would even
fall for such a woman [Dee Stanley]... He was at his most vulnerable, his
most honest, I would say his most passionate during that time."

22

A NEW HOBBY

In December 1959, Elvis began to intensify his commitment to a new hobby that would have a great influence on his life called karate. Elvis and Rex Mansfield first saw instructor Jürgen Seydel, known as the "father of German karate," at a local demonstration. They both started taking lessons with Seydel at his studio in Usingen in the spring around May or June of 1959. Elvis had become interested in karate while serving in Fort Hood.

"A part of Elvis' personality was looking for some discipline and order," explained Patsy Presley. "He didn't always achieve it, but he was always seeking it."

Since Elvis had some free time with his three-day pass in early December 1959, he asked Seydel to come over and give him private lessons at his home in Bad Nauheim. Elvis would continue these private lessons twice a week with Seydel until he returned to the States. They trained for three full hours at each session without a break. During this time, Seydel got to know Elvis fairly well on a personal level.

"Elvis was very willing to talk about all sorts of things," said Seydel. "When we were alone, we often talked about serious things like politics, parapsychology, character study and self-assessment. Sometimes we would sit and talk together until midnight."

Elvis saw learning karate as a challenge and he often chose Rex to be his sparring partner to do demonstrations in front of their friends. Elvis confided in Rex that karate gave him the confidence to defend himself in case his bodyguards like Red West were not around. For many years, Elvis kept his original karate test card from Seydel's school in his wallet, with the first test dated December 6, 1959.

"Elvis was athletic and well-trained, understood quickly, reacted coolly and precisely," described Seydel. "At his [Presley's] own request I grabbed him very hard and Elvis made amazing progress."

Meanwhile, at the end of November 1959, Presley had begun weekly skin treatments to reduce enlarged pores on his face and eliminate acne scars. In October, after seeing a magazine advertisement, Elvis contacted Dr. Laurenz Johannes Griessel-Landau, a supposed dermatologist, who claimed he had created a special formula that could do wonders for anti-aging of the skin. Elvis had been receiving the 10-week "Aroma Therapy" treatment at his home from this South African doctor for about a month when something disturbing happened.

"He was giving Elvis a massage on his face and his shoulders," recalled Lamar. "And all of a sudden, he eased his hand down between Elvis' legs and gave him a good squeeze. And, boy, Elvis jumped thirty feet up in the air."

Elvis let out a shriek and bolted out of the room. He accused Griessel-Landau of touching him inappropriately: "I'm going to kill the son of a bitch!" Elvis kept yelling. Lamar had to restrain Elvis, and the guys then proceeded to physically drag Landau out of the house.

Shockingly, Griessel-Landau returned to the house on Christmas Eve to ask Elvis when his next appointment would be. Elvis freaked out and started yelling at him and kicked him out of the house. But Griessel-Landau threatened to expose Presley's relationship with Priscilla and reveal photos and tape recordings of Elvis in "compromising situations" if he was not paid for the full 10-week treatment. However, Presley denied that any supposed photos or recordings of him in compromising situations existed.

When Vernon found out about the incident, he was quite upset. On December 26, he called The Colonel for advice. After making a few calls to his friends in the military, The Colonel instructed Elvis to report this attempt at blackmail to the army's Provost Marshal Division. On December 28, Elvis was interviewed by the Military Police. He told them that Griessel-Landau had made advances on his friends, but never admitted that Griessel-Landau had assaulted him. The case was referred to the FBI.

Elvis wanted to avoid any negative publicity, so he negotiated a payment for Griessel-Landau and agreed to buy him a plane ticket to

London. On January 6, 1960, Griessel-Landau, who did not have a medical degree after all, left Germany and never contacted Elvis again.

On the brighter side, things were getting serious between Elvis and Priscilla. While Elvis still saw other girls occasionally, Priscilla was the one he spent the most time with. She would come over to the house several times a week. But this was hard for Elisabeth to watch.

"I noticed Elvis treated her differently from all the other girls that he had been dating," Elisabeth described. "For example, when Priscilla was in the room, his entire attention was focused on her. I knew he felt strongly about Priscilla by the way he looked at her, sat next to her, whispered in her ear. Other girls were just part of the scenery around him."

With Elvis' attention focused on Priscilla, this gave Elisabeth a chance to date someone else, without Elvis knowing. That someone else was Rex Mansfield. However, it wasn't his or Elisabeth's idea to start dating – it was the last person you would expect: Presley's grandmother, Minnie Mae. When he was five years old, Elvis had nicknamed her "Dodger" for dodging her head out of the way from a baseball he had thrown that missed her head by just inches.

"Rex, you know that Elisabeth is a sweet person, and she'll make some man a good wife," Dodger told Rex in the fall of 1959.

If Elvis ever found out his own grandmother was plotting against him to set up his live-in "girlfriend" with one of his best friends, he would have been furious. But Dodger was a wise woman and didn't think it was right for Elvis to keep stringing loyal Elisabeth along as he dated countless other girls in front of her.

"That Rex Mansfield is such a nice young man, and he'll make some girl a good husband," Grandma told Elisabeth.

With Minnie Mae's encouragement, Rex and Elisabeth finally became convinced that it was worth risking Elvis' friendship to start dating each other. They would meet up at another friend's house in Bad Nauheim about twice a week. Eventually, Lamar and Cliff figured out the two were having a relationship behind Elvis' back but they agreed not to say anything. Elvis and Vernon were not aware of what was going on.

Meanwhile, back in the States, Colonel Parker sent out the annual Elvis Christmas cards with two pictures of Elvis that were taken in Bad Nauheim earlier that Spring. These cards were offered for free to any fan that came into the RCA Victor record stores.

Anticipating his return to life back in Memphis, Elvis arranged to send Anita Wood a unique Christmas gift of a guitar with an inscription on the front: "To Little, From EP." When Elvis returned home, he would play many songs on that guitar for Anita. For Christmas the year before, he scheduled a special delivery of a tiny white poodle to Anita so that she could "snuggle up to that little bitty thing" until he returned home.

In keeping with Presley's generous nature, especially around Christmas, it was reported in the newspapers that Elvis had donated $1500 for gifts and a party for the 115 German children in the Steinmuehle orphanage. "Never in the history of the orphanage has anyone treated the children so well," said the head of the orphanage.

In the meantime, Priscilla was agonizing over what to give Elvis for a Christmas present. She said the only thing she could afford was a pair of bongo drums. While money may have dictated her choice, a musical instrument couldn't help but build her bond with Elvis over their common interest in less mainstream types of music.

"Elvis was a big lover of opera," Priscilla explained. "When I met him in Germany, he practiced his voice every single night in preparation for serving his time and getting back into singing again, and operatic songs he would sing as well as other songs to prepare his voice."

On December 19, Presley's army battalion held a Christmas party at a local restaurant called Sportheim. This is believed to be the first time Elvis and Priscilla appeared together in public. There was a photo of them taken at the party where they are sitting side by side at a table. Presley's army buddy, Robert McDaniel, who was also a jeep driver in the platoon, and his wife Leona were at the Christmas party. They confirmed that Priscilla was there with Elvis. They even got their picture taken with Elvis that night. Elvis is pictured wearing a dark shirt with a brown blazer.

On Christmas day, Elvis threw a party at his home for family and friends. Vernon and Dee went to pick up Priscilla to bring her to the party. "Cilla was dressed very simply in a print dress with a high collar," Dee recalled, "and all of the other women were in low-cut things. She was the prettiest girl there, and Elvis couldn't take his eyes off her the whole night!"

Priscilla was elated when Elvis gave her a beautiful gold watch and pearl ring. "I'll cherish these forever," Priscilla told him. Elvis acted excited when Priscilla gave him the bongo drums, even though he already had a few sets stashed in his basement. Elvis then played the piano singing "I'll Be Home For Christmas" as Priscilla snuggled beside him.

"We had a Christmas party here," Elvis told Dick Clark in a live interview over the phone on January 8, 1960 for *American Bandstand*. "I had a lot of guys from all over the post, you know. I had as many of the boys here as possible at my house - try to make 'em feel at home around Christmas time... Then on New Year's night we had another little party."

Heli Priemel said she chose not to attend Presley's Christmas party at his home, but she did go to his New Year's Eve party. She says that Elvis gave a surprise private concert at a nondescript hall in Friedberg where Elvis sang 10 of his songs for an audience of about 100 soldiers, but Priscilla was not there.

Meanwhile, for his 25th birthday on January 8, Elvis threw a party at the local Bad Nauheim "Turnhalle" (gymnasium) recreation center with 150-200 guests including Priscilla. Joe Esposito and some of the other regular Sunday football players presented Elvis with a trophy which was inscribed: "Elvis Presley. Most Valuable Player. Bad Nauheim Sunday Afternoon Football Association, 1959."

At the party, Elvis was photographed feeding Priscilla a piece of cake. Heli says that she did not attend Elvis' birthday party because she was sick, but she would be attending one more event that Priscilla did not – Elvis' final trip to Paris.

Elvis had started a 13-day leave on January 5, 1960. After his birthday festivities, Presley traveled again to Paris for the last time on January 12 for five days. For this trip, he had a more productive reason for going. He wanted to advance his training in karate by studying with Seydel's former instructor, Tetsuji Murakami, a Japanese teacher of the Shotokan technique.

Seydel arranged the private training course at the Yoseikan karate studio for Presley, and he accompanied Elvis on the trip. Presley's other companions to Paris included Lamar Fike, Cliff Gleaves, Joe Esposito and Currie Grant. Elvis asked Rex Mansfield to go, but he declined so that he could secretly spend more time with Elisabeth.

While during the day from January 13 to 16, Presley trained in the special karate course with Murakami, at night he was back to his usual pastime of visiting multiple Paris nightclubs. He and his friends stayed at the Prince de Galles hotel again. The first night, Elvis hit the town in his army dress blue uniform with a black tie and white gloves. He was photographed at the Lido after the show talking to performer Harold Nicholas, who was part of the show. This African-American singer and dancer was part of the acclaimed tap dance duo, The Nicholas Brothers. While Elvis was waiting to see the twin performers, Alice and Ellen Kessler, whom he had met during his first trip to Paris, he was also photographed with a bunch of awestruck waiters and busboys at the club.

Joe Esposito had been assigned the duty of handling the expenses for Elvis while they were in Paris. He did such a good job that, before Elvis left the army, he asked Joe to come work for him back in Memphis. Meanwhile, during the trip, Joe Esposito was surprised to discover that Elvis refused to drink any alcohol. "I saw too many drunks in my youth," Elvis told him. "That's why you'll never see alcohol in my house. I do not accept it."

One French reporter, Arlette Gordon, who wrote for *Cinémonde* magazine, interviewed Elvis in his room, number 520, at the hotel. She described meeting Elvis: "A very thin, healthy and bright boy with short hair and a tanned complexion opens the door to me. With a mischievous smile and a green eye full of childish charm, he reaches out to me." She then described Elvis doing some karate moves for her, and then shows her a pile of books that he has acquired.

Obviously, Priscilla was too young to spend unchaperoned time in Paris. Instead, Elvis invited 16-year-old Heli to meet him there since she had missed Presley's birthday party. She came with her older sister, Isa-Vera Priemel, and they were both photographed at the Lido nightclub sitting at a table with Elvis and his friends including Joe Esposito, Cliff Gleaves, Jurgen Seydel, Currie Grant and Lamar. Heli says Elvis was wearing a wine-red tuxedo that night. She also remembered seeing the Kessler twins perform that night at the Lido, as well as a Swiss ventriloquist named Fred Roby.

Later, Currie drove home Heli's 21-year-old sister who was studying in Paris, while Cliff Gleaves took Heli back to the hotel. Elvis had reserved a room for her. When she heard a knock at the door, she expected to see Elvis.

However, things did not turn out exactly the way Heli would have liked. It was not Elvis at the door, but rather Joe Esposito, who had been sitting next to her all night at the Lido. Elvis was busy with the Kessler twins, so Heli did not get to spend that much time with him. Instead, Heli claims that Joe Esposito came into her hotel room and made a pass at her. She was not interested and warded off his advances. However, she did admit that she had a "nice friendship" with Cliff Gleaves and had been briefly involved with him.

Still fighting a cold and embarrassed to see Joe Esposito, Heli decided to leave Paris the next day. She left a note for Elvis. According to Heli, he called her that night and promised they would see each other before he left Germany. Heli was not aware that Elvis was also seeing another girl in Paris.

"There was a girl he particularly liked," Joe Esposito described. "Nancy Parker. I don't remember what show she was playing in. He liked her very much and he saw her two or three times... We saw the Eiffel Tower, Notre Dame... we did a lot of nightclubs. Several times the Crazy Horse Saloon. While dancing, all the girls looked at Elvis."

Another night, Elvis and the gang went to Casino de Paris to see The Golden Gate Quartet who were performing in the "Plaisirs" show (meaning "Pleasures" in English). The show was hosted by French female singer, Line Renaud. Renaud was alerted that Elvis was sitting in the balcony, so she requested that Elvis come backstage to meet her. Elvis was happy to do so, and asked if The Golden Gate Quartet could also be there. Renaud's husband, Loulou Gasté, immediately summoned the African-American gospel group to meet Elvis.

An article by columnist Carmen Tessier was published in the France-Soir newspaper on January 20 with the headline: "Elvis Presley improvises a 'jam session' in Line Renaud's dressing room at the Casino de Paris." Elvis sang gospel songs with the Quartet like "Down By The Riverside", "Swing Down, Sweet Chariot", and "When The Saints Go Marching In". The only people to hear this exclusive concert were Line Renaud, her husband, Renaud's hairdresser, her stylist, Presley's companions and the janitor of the theater.

"This began at midnight," Tessier wrote, "and at 4:00 in the morning, two enthusiastic spectators, Line Renaud and Loulou Gasté, could be seen applauding in a frenzy for Elvis Presley... He [Elvis] had grabbed Loulou's guitar, and in shirt sleeves, without a tie [he had removed his jacket] he sang accompanied by The Golden Gate Quartet, their entire repertoire."

"He played with his heart and soul," Renaud remembered. "He knew all the songs, you could feel it was his foundation, it was his classical music. There wasn't a Negro spiritual he didn't know. He knew them all by heart. As soon as he launched into something... sometimes it was the Quartet who started one and Elvis would join in. There was osmosis, it was extraordinary."

"It was great!" said Clyde Wright, a member of the group. "Elvis is a charming boy."

That night in Paris was such a memorable night for Elvis since he had been a huge fan of the group since his early childhood. The quartet, which had many rotating members over the years, was originally founded in 1934 and was originally called The Golden Gate Jubilee Quartet. Elvis would later record several gospel songs previously recorded by the group including "Swing Down, Sweet Chariot", "I Will Be Home Again", "Joshua Fit The Battle of Jericho", "I Was Born Ten Thousand Years Ago" and many more.

"It was an extraordinary experience with The Golden Gate Quartet," Joe Esposito reminisced about the Paris trip. "Elvis loved them because he loved gospel music and was delighted to meet them because they were famous as well... Line Renaud, a wonderful woman. We had a very good time watching her show. Elvis appreciated good artists, good singers and all the artists we saw..."

On January 17, 1960, Presley left Paris for the third and final time. He was followed by photographers as he and his friends left the hotel on their way to the railway station. Elvis is photographed talking with an unidentified blonde woman as he walks through the station. He finally boards his train headed for Germany which leaves at 10:05 p.m.

Visiting the City of Lights was definitely one of the most memorable experiences Presley had in the army. In later years, the Prince de Galles Hotel would promote their association with Elvis with the slogan: "Live like the King at the Prince."

"It was just wonderful. I had a great time," Presley declared. "If you want to have fun, you've got to see Paris."

Elvis did very well with his martial arts training in Paris. Master Murakami was impressed at how serious and talented Elvis was in karate. He told Seydel that if Elvis trained for one to two more months, he could reach a performance level of 3 Kyu, which usually required up to two years of training for most students.

"He had an incredible capacity for perception and was one of my most talented pupils," said Seydel about Elvis.

On March 1, 1960, right before Elvis left Germany, Seydel presented Elvis with a certificate of achievement in karate. At the end it read: "The above-average achievements and the extensive coverage of the principles of Budo leave me to prematurely award the 3rd Kyu Karate to Mr. Presley. He is therefore entitled to wear the brown belt."

Elvis was so happy and proud to have received his brown belt in karate that he wrote his instructor a gracious letter, and also gifted him the red Volkswagen he had originally bought for Lamar and Red West to use.

"Dear Mr. Seydel 'George,'

I wish to thank you from the bottom of my heart for taking the time to teach me the basic steps of 'Karate.' You have been very patient in teaching me and I want you to know that I have learned a lot and that I am very satisfied. This little gift is not a payment for the lessons, but just to show my appreciation for your time and patience. Thanking you again. I am your friend,

Elvis Presley / 3rd Cue [Kyu] Karate"

This was just the start for Elvis' love of karate and his lifelong ritual of practicing every day. In later years, Presley became so dedicated to practicing karate that Red West said, "Elvis' whole life is singing and karate. In that order."

"It's a way of life, not something that you use to beat people up with," Elvis described. "It's so much more than a sport. It teaches discipline, patience, and makes you more spiritual."

23

MEDIA-FRENZIED MANEUVERS

On January 20, 1960, just three days after his return from Paris, Elvis was promoted to Acting Sergeant. Advancing from his role as a scout-jeep driver, Presley was now a squad leader commanding a three-man reconnaissance team of his own, which he would run for the Seventh Army's upcoming "Winter Shield" maneuvers. The team consisted of Elvis, his driver and a machine-gunner.

"He's earned the job," said Presley's platoon leader, First Lieutenant Richard L. Coffman. "I'd be glad to have him in my platoon any time."

The new title earned Elvis a third stripe on his uniform. According to an army official, Presley was named to fill a squad leader's vacancy before the promotion allocation came down "because we need right away a good man to do the job."

Two days later on January 22, Elvis got a medical checkup by the army. It was a revealing look at Presley's health history, showing that the 25-year-old had experienced childhood illnesses including mumps and whooping cough. It also validated the claims by friends and family that Elvis had "been a sleep walker," and that he had "frequent trouble sleeping" and "terrifying nightmares."

Presley reported for Operation Winter Shield on Sunday, January 24. It was the Seventh Army's annual winter maneuver staged in the vicinity of Grafenwoehr. For this 14-day NATO exercise, 60,000 troops and 15,000 vehicles took part. It marked the first time that major units of the new German Army participated in a field exercise with U.S. ground forces.

This was the most "intense and crucial" training exercise that Elvis and Rex had participated in during their army service. According to Rex, Operation Winter Shield was "designed to test our combat readiness as well as to train us in extreme cold conditions." The weather was so cold that it was common for soldiers to get frostbite and have to be sent to the hospital.

As a leader of a scout patrol, Presley and his team would move in advance of the troops and tanks to check for signs of the enemy and check roads and bridges for maneuverability. He would use field maps to plan his route and coordinate strategies with other team leaders on the radio. The reconnaissance teams like Presley's were the "eyes and ears" of the 32nd Armor Regiment.

There were about 150 members of the European and American press who took part in observing the maneuvers, which were so important since they simulated the use of atomic weapons in war. Several members of the press came determined to get an exclusive story with Acting Sergeant Presley out in the field, but few were able to locate Elvis. One reporter described their pursuit when they finally found Elvis on his knees changing a tire in the snow. When they asked Presley to do an interview, Elvis replied: "Nah. Don't want interviews." Refusing to give up, the journalists kept cajoling Elvis, when finally the word came from Major General Frederic Brown: "Sergeant Presley will not be interviewed now. Period."

When the soldiers were out in the field on maneuvers, they would often park the jeeps and tanks in the woods in areas outside small towns. This provided a chance for German Elvis fans to seek out their idol. In a rare occasion, another American soldier was mistaken for Elvis by the fans. Private First Class John Gilgun, who served with Elvis both at Fort Hood and in Friedberg, says that one time during maneuvers, a fellow soldier pointed a group of young German fans in his direction. Surprisingly, even though Gilgun had no facial resemblance to Presley (although he was thin and tall like Elvis) Presley's fans rushed over to Gilgun, who was a tank driver.

"They asked for autographs and I signed every one that was put in front of me — 'Elvis Presley.' To this day, there are probably people in Germany who think they have an Elvis Presley autograph but they have a John Gilgun autograph," he said with a chuckle. "It was fun just writing his name and seeing those kids running off, thrilled, thinking they had seen Elvis."

One of Presley's duties was to be stationed at an entry point where he directed tanks and support vehicles into an area where the troops would take turns resting for a day. The area was a makeshift shelter with no tents or cover. Although Rex and Elvis did not see much of each other during those two weeks, the long hours and miserable weather were the reason they both agreed this was the worst experience of their entire time in the army.

But even so, Elvis still found some relief towards the end of the training. On Friday, February 5, while Presley and his team were waiting for a group of tanks to arrive, they stopped in the town of Hirschau. Elvis walked into a shop to buy cigarettes for his two companions. The shop assistant said he recognized Elvis as he was trying to use the vending machine.

The news quickly spread that Elvis was there. Edith Luhmann, an apprentice in the shop across the street, said it was around 1:30 p.m. when someone told them that Elvis was in town. Presley's jeep was parked next to the church. He was there with two fellow soldiers including Sergeant First Class Billy G. Wilson.

Elvis visited the market square where he was quickly surrounded by a hoard of people. Rudi Wild, a young boy who stood in the crowd of young girls around Elvis, remarked: "I had no chance myself. I was a kid of 12 years. And at 12 years, you can't push the girls away so that you can get close to Elvis."

Elvis was quite interested in the DKW sports car that was parked on the street. It was owned by Sepp Anderl Müller, a reporter with the local newspaper *Amberger Zeitung*. When Müller found out who was admiring his car, he came outside and talked with Elvis. He even let Elvis get in the car. Although he was not an Elvis fan, Müller was impressed by the modesty and friendly nature of the famous star.

Realizing what a great opportunity had fallen into his lap, Müller asked Elvis if he could interview him and Elvis agreed. The crowd then followed Elvis and Sepp Muller with camera on-hand into The Golden Lamb ("Goldenes Lamm") pub around 3 p.m. Many young kids made it inside before the management realized what was happening.

Elvis had a coke and his colleagues drank beer. The teenage fans got Elvis to sign his autograph on the back of the pub's coasters which were labeled "Lowen-Brau Grafenwoehr." Twelve-year-old Dagmar Kiermeier got into the pub with her girlfriend and went right up to Elvis sitting at the round table.

"He took me and put me on his lap," Dagmar recalled. "I would have sat there until today, of course!"

Meanwhile, as the pub became overcrowded, people started waiting outside to get a glimpse of Elvis. Inside, the teenagers asked him to sing, but Presley gestured no, by running his hand undercutting his neck. Elvis had a constant stream of young girls surrounding him. A few times when the young girls got too close, Presley "reached for his coke bottle, working his way out of an awkward situation." Nevertheless, Getrud Wetzchewald got a picture of her kissing Elvis' cheek.

"He was sitting there in front of his coke, relaxed, and seemed to have enjoyed all the women around him," explained Lieselotte Zelenka, a young girl who also got in the pub. "And then he put his finger under my chin and there is a picture [of it]."

After about four hours, Elvis finally had to leave. There were pictures taken outside when it was dark showing people milling around Elvis as he departed. Elvis and some other soldiers even had a playful snowball fight with some of the Hirschau girls. Presley shook people's hands and said goodbye to them in German: "Auf Wiedersehen," he said.

During Presley's visit at the pub, Müller was able to interview Elvis and take 12 photos of him with the fans. Müller's story was published in a local German newspaper a few days later with the headline: (translated) "Elvis was now 'snapped': In Hirschau he could no longer maintain his incognito." In the interview, Elvis stated that he was quite surprised to find out that his fame and popularity had reached this far corner of Bavaria. "But the people are nice here," he said.

Elvis told Sepp that he was really looking forward to returning home in about 23 days, when his army service would be completed. He then asked Sepp to send him the photos that he took of Elvis with his young teenage fans. Sepp sent the photos addressed to "Elvis Presley, Graceland USA." A few months later, Sepp received a thank-you letter from Elvis.

Sepp was one of the few journalists to get time with Elvis in the Upper Palatinate district of Bavaria, Germany. His recollection of Presley that day in Hirschau was bittersweet: "Presley may have had mountains of money," the journalist explained. "But because of his popularity, he couldn't cross the street without a crowd. That is real poverty."

A few days later on February 8, two soldiers from another platoon, Specialists Fourth Class Ford and Hightower, brought a special fan to meet

Elvis out on the field. Possibly captured roaming in the Bavarian forest, a young lioness with a chain collar was held by Ford as a group of soldiers crowded around Elvis for autographs. Of course, Elvis had a lifelong love for animals, but he seemed a bit taken aback in the photos as the lioness was growling.

On Thursday, February 11, 1960, right before the Winter Shield maneuvers were over, Elvis was promoted to Sergeant. He was presented with the stripes by Lieutenant Colonel Jones in Grafenwoehr. Although Elvis had been wearing his three "acting sergeant" stripes during the maneuvers, it was now official.

Similar to Presley's rapid advancement to Private First Class in November 1958, this was an unusual promotion to level E-5 or "Buck Sergeant" for a draftee to receive so quickly when he had only been serving for just under two years. According to military sources, soldiers usually earn the rank of Specialist (E-4) after having served a minimum of two years. But under the circumstances, Presley's superiors obviously thought he was doing an exceptional job.

Considering all the skepticism that accompanied Elvis when he was first inducted into the army, the fact that he was promoted to Sergeant was a huge accomplishment. One reporter observed: "Only a tiny proportion of draftees ever manage such a promotion, and had you been asked in the summer of 1958 to name one soldier in the whole of the United States armed forces for whom this would not have been possible, you would have been right in saying Elvis.".

Not only was Elvis proud on a professional level, but also on a personal level since his buddy Rex Mansfield had been promoted to sergeant before him. Up to that point, they had been promoted to each higher rank at the same time, but Rex was a tank commander and had been promoted to sergeant one month before Elvis. Elvis was jealous and even claimed that Rex was only promoted because he was Presley's friend. It caused such tension that Rex would not wear his uniform (with the three stripes) when visiting Elvis in Bad Nauheim.

So when Elvis finally got his sergeant stripes it was especially a relief to Rex. When Elvis returned home to Bad Nauheim, he threw a small party to celebrate. Just a week later, Presley received an impressive Letter of Commendation from Lieutenant Colonel Jones dated February 19, 1960 which surely added to Presley's sense of pride and accomplishment. Here is an excerpt:

"Your unselfish and uncomplaining attitude has been of direct benefit in maintaining the high morale prevalent in the platoon. Your refusal to trade up your professional reputation in any manner whatsoever should be a source of great pride to you. You have shared the bad times and the good times with your associates in a manner which has earned the respect and admiration of every soldier with whom you served. Your promotions have been honestly and fairly won in competition with all others."

24

ROMANCE LEAKED BY UNLIKELY SOURCE

On February 26, 1960, about two weeks after being promoted to Sergeant, Elvis finally got the official news he had been waiting 17 months to hear. His official redeployment notice stated that he would be returning to the States and would be transferred to Fort Dix, New Jersey on March 3. As a result, Elvis could start finalizing his plans to leave Germany.

With all the media interest in Elvis, it was almost a miracle that no one in the press had found out about Priscilla up to that point. But that would soon change.

What had been a well-kept secret for over five months among Elvis Presley's close friends and family was suddenly broadcast to the world on March 1, 1960. The news came out that in Germany, Elvis had been dating an American teenager, Priscilla Beaulieu, for several months. However, the news reports incorrectly stated she was 16 years old.

Presley and his entourage had done such a great job of keeping Priscilla's relationship with Elvis a secret since September 1959. In fact, Presley could have left Germany with that secret kept hidden. The only exception was the threat of exposure by the South African "doctor" a few months prior, but that was no longer an issue.

Keeping quiet would have been the smart thing to do since it would have saved Elvis from suspicion by his Memphis girlfriend, Anita Wood, and would also avoid controversy relating to the fact that Priscilla was so young. So enquiring minds want to know: Who was the culprit that betrayed Elvis and Priscilla's privacy?

It is shocking to reveal that the person who first "leaked" the news is the last person you would expect - it was Elvis Presley himself!

Presley spilled the beans to British journalist Peter Hopkirk. Hopkirk had been trying for months to get an exclusive story on Elvis. He was surprised when Elvis called him over for an impromptu interview on Monday, February 29.

On the day of the interview, Hopkirk was accompanied by photographer James Whitmore at Presley's home to take photos of Elvis packing his bags for his upcoming departure of Germany two days later. He also posed with the Certificate of Achievement he received on February 24. It read: Awarded to Sergeant Elvis A. Presley "in recognition of faithful and efficient performance of duty and for outstanding service to the US Army from October 1, 1958 to February 15, 1960".

In this spontaneous interview with Hopkirk, Elvis could not help but gush about Priscilla: "There is only one reason why I shall be sorry to leave here," Presley revealed, "and that is Priscilla. Hardly anyone knows about us. She is only 16. But she's very mature. And intelligent."

As evident in the interview, Elvis was the one who planted the falsehood that Priscilla was two years older than she actually was. During the interview, Hopkirk described Elvis as picking up Priscilla's picture and whistling at it, saying: "I think she's the most beautiful girl I've ever seen. I've dated plenty of girls while I've been here, both German and American, but Priscilla's definitely the sharpest of them."

"Serious? I think I've said enough already," Presley continued. "But it's a pity she won't be coming back to America for a while." (Priscilla's father was stationed in Germany for another two years.)

As Hopkirk realized he had just broken a huge story, Presley grinned and said: "I shall be in trouble tomorrow for talking to you." Sure enough, Hopkirk would state in his article: "Sergeant Elvis Presley let me into a little secret tonight."

Hopkirk immediately wrote his article later that day entitled "Presley's Secret...It's Priscilla: Only 16 but oh so very sharp!" and submitted it to his paper, *The Daily Express*, in London. The photo which appeared with the article shows Priscilla dressed-up wearing a black and white top. The next day on Tuesday, March 1, 1960, this article - which broke the news to the world about Priscilla - was published in the early morning.

Once word got out through Hopkirk's article, that gave reporters a chance to ask Elvis about Priscilla later that morning. During a press conference held by the army on March 1 at the enlisted men's club in Friedberg, Germany, Elvis was asked about a romance with Air Force Captain Paul Beaulieu's 16-year-old daughter, Priscilla.

"Yes," Elvis responded to a group of over 100 journalists. "She's about sixteen, but she's very mature for her years. I'm very fond of her, but she's just a friend. There's no big romance."

"She is very mature," Elvis continued. "She's got beautiful blue eyes. A very pretty brunette and I like her very much."

It was such an eye-popping story that it made headlines in newspapers all across the U.S. The A.P. story on March 2, 1960 called attention to the fact that Elvis was leaving his 16-year-old girlfriend behind in Germany. Presley also told reporters they had been dating three to four months and they spent time at her father's home, going to the movies and going for rides together.

Just a few days earlier, on February 26, Elvis had called his girlfriend in Memphis, Anita Wood, in anticipation of his return. Why he would divulge his relationship with Priscilla just a few days later is quite surprising. He knew it would make the papers and that Anita Wood would find out.

Not to mention that Presley's confession thrust Priscilla into the limelight. Once reporters got confirmation from Elvis about Priscilla at the press conference on March 1, they got in contact with her father first, and then her by interviewing her over the phone. The Associated Press made arrangements to come take pictures of her immediately following the press conference that same day.

The next day, Wednesday, March 2, a photo of Priscilla dressed in a white blouse and beige sweater holding an "action" shot of Elvis in the army was printed along with the AP article in a multitude of newspapers in the U.S. with headlines like: "Elvis Returning to U.S., Bids Girlfriend Good-Bye" and "Presley to Leave Date, 16, Fly Home." Imagine how this 14-year-old unknown girl felt then practically becoming a household name overnight.

"I am very fond of him," Priscilla told a reporter over the phone from the High School for United States Dependents at Wiesbaden Air Base, "but you shouldn't think there is anything serious."

"I'm too young for marriage," Priscilla explained, "but I think Elvis is a wonderful boy - so kind, so considerate, and such a gentleman. He gives a girl anything she could possible wish for."

In a shrewd move that seemed like Elvis had taken on a new role as his own publicist, Elvis also revealed at the press conference that Priscilla may be at the airport the following day when he departed Germany. When contacted by the press on March 1, Priscilla confirmed that yes, she would be there. The press could not have asked for a better photo op.

In a March 2 article entitled "Elvis to fly to US today; Priscilla yearns for kiss," Priscilla said about Elvis: "He is very intelligent, he's wonderful, he's charming. We kissed, that's all… I hope I can kiss him good-by tomorrow."

The evening of March 1, Elvis had a small farewell party at his house. This would be Elvis and Priscilla's last night together before Presley had to board the plane back to the U.S. At the party, Elvis asked Currie Grant and his wife, Carol, to bring Priscilla back to Bad Nauheim the following morning. Priscilla would return home later that night and return in the morning to accompany Elvis to the airport.

Priscilla was in panic mode wondering if this would be the last time she would ever see Elvis. He tried to reassure her: "I'm not going to forget you, Cilla. I've never felt this way about another girl. I love you… I'm torn with the feelings I have for you. I don't know what to do. Maybe being away will help me understand what I really feel."

The morning of March 2 when Elvis came downstairs ready to leave his Bad Nauheim house for the last time, there were many people waiting to say goodbye to him, including many of the other girls Elvis had dated during his time in Germany. Heli von Westrem says she was waiting amongst a bunch of other people who were crowded in the living room and hallway. She says Elvis spotted her and walked over to her with his latest LP to give to her. Heli asked him to sign it. He wrote: "To Heli, Best of Luck, Always, From Elvis Presley."

As Heli described, it was an "innocuous" greeting, which seemed to symbolize her fading connection with Elvis – something that Heli was not ready to accept. He gave her a "short, loving" hug and then she left. "Little did I know that we would never see each other again," Heli recalled.

When Presley came out of the front door of his home, of course there were more people outside waiting to say goodbye to The King of Rock and Roll. One of them was 17-year-old Roswitha Klaus who had started dating Elvis over a year earlier. She was broken-hearted that Elvis was leaving. She watched as Elvis was photographed getting into a car with another girl named Priscilla. Roswitha did not realize how serious it was between them.

"Without a long goodbye, he just drove off," Roswitha recalled. "I never saw him again."

A few days earlier, Presley had thrown a large party inviting lots of friends, both male and female, to his home. Surprisingly, Margit Buergin was at the party. She said her final goodbye to Elvis that night.

After saying his goodbyes in front of his home, Elvis, with only Priscilla at his side, was driven to Ray Barracks by The Grants so Elvis could say a final goodbye to his fellow soldiers. During the ride, Elvis gave Priscilla his combat jacket with his new Sergeant stripes and said, "I want you to have these. It shows you belong to me." Then, he held her tight.

At the barracks, Elvis and Priscilla parted ways. Elvis was taken to the airport by secured military transport, and Priscilla was driven there separately. Priscilla reflected on what Elvis had told her in the car: "I want you to promise me you'll stay the way you are – untouched, just as I left you."

The press had a field day at the Rhein-Main Air Base in Frankfurt that afternoon taking pictures not only of Elvis, but also Priscilla. Before they parted, Elvis had asked Priscilla to smile at the airport even though she was extremely upset. That is why Priscilla appears relatively calm and happy in the photographs taken of her at the airport gates, even though she was devastated inside.

"I'll look for you from the top of the ramp," Elvis told Priscilla. "I don't want to see a sad face. Give me a little smile. I'll take that with me."

When Elvis boarded the plane, Priscilla was upset that she did not get to have one final goodbye with him. In addition, the army was upset because the public relations focus had shifted from the theme of the departure of Elvis "the soldier" to the departure of Elvis "the lover".

The topic of Priscilla dating Elvis in Germany was not taken seriously by Anita Wood when Elvis returned home. Elvis told her, "It's all for publicity, nothing's going on" and that Priscilla "happened to be a huge fan," and that was the end of it as far as Anita was concerned.

"I had read a little bit about Priscilla in the papers and he assured me that this was a child," Anita explained in 2012. "A 14-year-old child that was the daughter of an Army Officer… He wrote me three letters [from Germany] that were very special to me and to anybody that would read them. He swore he loved me, how we would get married, how there was no one else, how I needed to stay true to him and remain and wait for him."

After all the passionate letters Elvis had sent her, Anita had no reason to doubt his love for her. When Elvis returned to Memphis in March 1960, they picked up where they had left off with their relationship and continued dating for another two years.

However, the revelation that Elvis leaked his romance with Priscilla is a testament to how taken he was with her.

"If you've ever heard of love at first sight, that had to be what that was," said Presley's army buddy, Rex Mansfield, recalling when Elvis first met Priscilla. "Because I've never seen him act like he did toward her. He was just going, 'Oh, she's a little angel. That's the most beautiful girl I've ever seen in my life."

Of course, Elvis downplayed the romance when asked about it a week after he left Germany at a press conference at Graceland on March 7, 1960:

Reporter: "How about any romance - did you leave any hearts, shall we say, in Germany?"

Elvis: "(Laughs) Not any special one, no. There was a little girl that I was seeing quite often over there that... her father was in the Air Force. Actually, they only got over there about two months before I left. I was seeing her and she was at the train - at the airport when I left. And there were some pictures made of her (laughs). But it was no big, it was no big romance. I mean the stories came out 'The Girl He Left Behind' (laughs) and all that. It wasn't like that, I mean (laughs). I have to be careful when I answer a question like that (laughs)."

"At the [Memphis] press conference when Elvis said, 'No, there wasn't anyone special,' my heart sank," Priscilla described years later. "But then when he said, 'Yes, there was someone,' my heart leaped. He didn't have to say that. Elvis never said anything he didn't want to say. I understood his concern about his public image. I knew how cautious and private he was about acknowledging any sort of romance. So when he said 'yes,' in spite of his qualifications, I knew he was thinking of me."

Even *LIFE* magazine featured an article in their March 14, 1960 issue which ran the headline "Farewell to Priscilla, Hello to U.S.A." In the article, a photo of Priscilla had the caption "Girl He Left Behind." It showed a photo of Elvis and Priscilla in the car together as he was being driven to the airport on March 2. She was also photographed waving to Elvis from the crowd as he got onto the plane.

The week Elvis returned to the U.S., Priscilla was photographed again in Germany standing by a record player holding the Presley album *For LP Fans Only* and sitting at a desk like she was writing a letter to Elvis. The "Farewell Letter to Elvis" picture appeared in papers around the country starting March 5. Part of the caption read: "She has been Elvis' steady date for the past six weeks." The other photograph where she was standing by the record player started appearing in papers on March 10. This photo's caption stated Priscilla had been dating Elvis for six months.

Elvis and Priscilla did not see each other again for two years. They kept in touch by phone and Priscilla constantly wrote letters to Elvis, although he never wrote back.

"He wasn't a letter writer but he would send me records as personal messages," Priscilla explained. "Sometimes they were his records and sometimes songs sung by others. The titles said it all: 'I'll Take Good Care of You,' 'Soldier Boy,' 'It's Now or Never,' 'Fever'."

Even though Elvis was the one who originally let the cat out of the bag, another reason he downplayed their relationship to the press was because he did not know when he would see Priscilla again.

"Two years passed," Priscilla recalled. "Two torturous years. Two years during which he maintained unpredictable contact. When I didn't hear from him, I was heartbroken. When I did, I was ecstatic. Finally he said the words I wanted to hear: 'I have to see you.'" Elvis and Priscilla finally reunited in June 1962 when Elvis sent Priscilla a plane ticket to Los Angeles.

But in leaking news of the romance when he left Germany – which some might say was passive aggressive behavior – Elvis let it be known to the world that he cared for Priscilla and that she was a contender for his heart.

25

WELCOME HOME, ELVIS!

With a wave goodbye to Priscilla, Elvis boarded the plane at the Rhein-Main Air Base near Frankfurt on March 2, 1960 to return back to the United States. Elvis had all of his belongings shipped home separately, including about 2,000 records that he had acquired while in Germany – many sent from his friends in Memphis and RCA contacts.

The plane left at 5:25 p.m. and stopped for a refueling in Prestwick, Scotland in the early morning hours of March 3 – the only time Elvis would ever step foot in the U.K. Word spread fast that Elvis would be stopping there. As a result, a bunch of fans were waiting for him even though it was after midnight. Elvis got off the plane for two hours and went to the U.S. Air Force reception hall at the airport. He gave a few informal interviews and then signed autographs for fans inside and outside.

Two days before, on March 1, Elvis ran into an old friend at his final press conference in Germany at the army base in Friedberg. It was Marion Keisker – now Captain Marion Keisker. Three years after helping Sam Phillips launch Presley's career at Sun Studio, she had left the music industry which she described as one of the "filthiest, dirtiest, back-stabbingest" businesses that she had ever been involved with.

Marion had a falling out with Sam Phillips and left Sun Studio in 1957. She decided to join the Air Force to see the world. She was soon stationed in Germany as an information officer for the Armed Forces television station at the Ramstein Air Base, which was less than two hours from Friedberg. Air Force Captain Keisker had come in official capacity that day to cover Presley's press conference.

When Elvis saw her dressed in uniform, he was extremely surprised, and exclaimed: "Do I kiss you or salute you?"

"In that order," she replied, and then gave Elvis a big hug.

At the press conference, a reporter asked Presley if his army experience had been beneficial to him in any way. Elvis replied: "It's been a big help in both my career and my personal life, because I learned a lot, I made a lot of friends that I never would have made otherwise, and I've had a lot of good experiences... and some bad ones, naturally. It's good to rough it, to put yourself to a test, to see if you can take it, to see if you can stand it."

The next day during his long flight to the U.S., Presley was awarded a service ribbon for Good Conduct. He could be seen wearing it for the first time when he arrived at 7:42 a.m. on March 3 in the middle of a snowstorm at McGuire Air Force Base in New Jersey. Even in the snow, Presley got a warm welcome from the media and also many fans who were trying to get a glimpse of their rock and roll hero as he arrived back in America. After Elvis went through customs, the army held a huge press conference for Presley - the first in almost 18 months on U.S. soil.

Colonel Parker, Jean Aberbach and many RCA reps were there to greet Elvis. Also, Nancy Sinatra was there to welcome Elvis home on behalf of her father. In just a few weeks, on March 26, Elvis would tape *The Frank Sinatra Timex Show: Welcome Home Elvis* TV special with Sinatra in Miami, which would later air on May 12.

A reporter asked Elvis if he was "apprehensive about what must be a comeback." Elvis replied: "Yes, I am. I mean I have my doubts... The only thing I can say is that I'm gonna try. I'll be in there fighting."

After the press conference, Elvis would spend the next two days at Fort Dix going through routine discharge procedures. He was released on the morning of March 5 at 9:15 a.m. with an honorable discharge. Elvis would serve the rest of his time on "reserve status." Since he would have to travel for his career, he was put on stand-by, where he would only be called up as part of an emergency. He was officially discharged from the Army Reserve on February 29, 1964.

After leaving Fort Dix, Elvis took a long train ride back to Memphis in a private railway car (with a transfer in Washington DC) accompanied by Colonel Parker, Parker's assistant Tom Diskin, Parker's brother-in-law Bitsy Mott, Rex Mansfield and Lamar Fike. He spoke with a few reporters on the train and stepped onto the observation platform to wave to fans during stops. For this special occasion of his return, Elvis was wearing his formal dress blues. However, there was something wrong with his uniform. He was wearing four stripes, which represented the rank of Staff Sergeant, instead of three, which was Presley's actual rank as Sergeant.

"I'll probably get put in jail about that," Elvis told a reporter. "It was a tailor's mistake in Germany. We had a rush job on it the last day I was there. I called and told him to sew on Sergeant's stripes and he added a fourth stripe."

Upon his arrival at Union Station in Memphis at 7:45 a.m. on March 7, Presley was greeted by a multitude of fans including Gary Pepper and his mother Nell who founded The Tankers Fan Club in honor of Elvis serving in the tank division. For the 20-minute ride back to Graceland, Elvis, The Colonel and Bitsy Mott were chauffeured in a police car driven by Memphis Police Captain Fred Woodward.

Meanwhile, Presley's father and grandmother along with Dee Stanley and Elisabeth Stefaniak were flying back to Memphis on a commercial airline. Elvis had asked Elisabeth to come work for him at Graceland, unaware that she was now dating Rex. Her stepfather had been redeployed back to the States to Fort Campbell, Kentucky, so Elisabeth agreed to fly to Graceland to help Minnie Mae, who had been sick the last week, to return home safely. Elisabeth was torn as to whether she should continue working for Elvis. However, when they got to Memphis, Elvis made her decision easy.

A few days after he returned to Graceland, Elvis took Elisabeth for a motorcycle ride. He told her that he had "lifted her restrictions," meaning he would allow her to date other people. On March 11, Elvis gave her a yellow Lincoln Continental, and personally helped her practice driving – something he could have easily asked one of the guys to do. Elisabeth was thrilled, but she was also disappointed and confused.

"I finally figured out that Elvis was trying to let me down as gently as possible," Elisabeth explained. "Things were suddenly becoming very clear in my mind. In staying with Elvis, I would only be his private secretary. I could leave with Rex and be his one and only. That was it – my mind was made up."

As Elvis resumed his relationship with Anita, Elisabeth and Rex were now planning their life together. Elvis had asked Rex to come work for him as well, but Rex realized that if he and Elisabeth wanted to be together, they would have to get away from Presley's world. On March 15, Rex and Elisabeth left Graceland separately, only to meet up later at the Memphis airport. Rex told Elvis he would be returning home to start work. Elisabeth left on the pretense that she was going away to visit her parents. As far as Elvis knew, Elisabeth would be returning to Graceland.

The couple that Minnie Mae helped put together went to say their real goodbyes to her before they both left Graceland for good. They got an unwelcome response: "Rex and Elisabeth, I urge you to confess your sins to Elvis," Grandma told them.

But Rex and Elisabeth did not want a confrontation with Elvis. While most of Presley's entourage knew how serious it was between Rex and Elisabeth, at that point, Elvis only had an inkling. As Elisabeth was getting ready to be driven to the airport by none other than Janie Wilbanks, Elvis confronted her at Graceland and asked her if she was going to be with Rex. (He was apparently tipped off by Cliff Gleaves.) Elisabeth said "no."

Rex and Elisabeth never returned to Graceland, and they ended up getting married on June 4, 1960. They sent Elvis an invitation to their wedding, but never got a response. Neither of them ever saw Elvis again.

Meanwhile, the first day Elvis arrived back in Memphis on March 7, he held a press conference in his father's office in a small building behind Graceland. The press conference lasted for about 15 minutes. Elvis talked about what was the hardest part about being in the army:

"Just being away from show business altogether. That was the hardest part of all. It wasn't the Army. It wasn't the other men. It was that. It stayed on my mind. I kept thinking about the past all the time, contemplating the future, and that was the hardest part... Someone asked me this morning 'what did I miss about Memphis,' and I said 'everything.'"

The next day on March 8, Presley went to visit his mother's grave at Forest Hill Cemetery. It was the first time he had seen the marker and stone angels that were placed there. Elvis had fresh flowers sent to her grave every week until the day he died.

"It was a time of grief for me," Elvis recalled about his army service. "It came at a time when I sorely needed a change. God's hand at work. The army took me away from myself and gave me something different."

With all the fear The King of Rock and Roll had about going into the army, it surprisingly may have been the best thing for his career. Being removed from the limelight seemed to work to Presley's advantage following Colonel Parker's management strategy of "less is more" - the less the public had access to you, the more in demand you were.

As a result, the two years of Elvis serving his country turned out to be the best free publicity he could have ever gotten - setting him up for even bigger movie and recording deals than he had before being drafted. Due in part to Colonel Parker's negotiation skills, Presley was a much more viable commodity when he got out of the army. Presley's return was so highly anticipated that he earned $125,000 for appearing only eight minutes on Frank Sinatra's show, which was more than Sinatra did for hosting the entire one-hour episode.

It truly was two years that changed Presley's life in many ways. When Presley went into the army, he was a rebellious 23-year-old with the world at his feet. He had two parents and a demanding manager watching over him. But for almost two years, Presley had been without his mother and was more independent without Colonel Parker around. Now 25 years old, Presley returned to the States with a newly found confidence reflected in his personal and professional life.

"When Elvis came back from Germany, I saw a much more mature guy," recalled George Klein. "At first, we thought the army situation was kind of a bad deal for him, but now I look back on it and think it kind of brought him back down to earth."

Being away from the music industry allowed Presley's true musical passions to blossom. In the early days of his career, Elvis did not intentionally choose rock and roll – rock and roll chose him. Now as a successful artist, Presley had the freedom to let his musical style evolve which would be reflected on his first post-army album, *Elvis Is Back!*, and the accompanying singles like "It's Now or Never."

"He now sang more from the diaphragm – with twice the vocal power of his rockabilly days," explained Billy Smith. Or as Elvis put it: "It's the same music, but with more balls." Presley's instincts would again be proven right. "It's Now or Never" would become Presley's biggest-selling single ever with international sales surpassing the 20-million mark.

Speaking about his army experience to British journalist, Peter Hopkirk, Elvis said: "I wouldn't have missed it for anything. I think it will prove to have assisted my career, especially as an actor. I'm much more mature now."

Elvis was in no hurry to let his sideburns grow back either. He even admitted in 1956 that he was getting tired of them but was afraid to change his look at that point. Also, his clothing tastes had changed after being in the service, as he loved to parade around in his uniform. He was also influenced by seeing Parisian fashions up close.

The rock and roll rebel had evolved into a suave gentleman, which coincidentally aligned with his main career goal. Colonel Parker was proven right in that army service could work to his client's advantage. In the eyes of the mainstream public, Elvis now had more respectability among the establishment and had widened his fan base.

"I want to be more of an actor and less of a singer," Presley told reporters. "My dream is still to have a career like Frank Sinatra's, who worked his way up from a crooner to a serious actor."

On a personal level, his love for karate took hold while he was in the army. It would become a huge part of his life from then on. Charlie Hodge and Joe Esposito, who he both met during the service, would join his entourage. Meeting Priscilla would also change his personal life in the years to come. In 1967, he and Priscilla would get married and they would have a daughter named Lisa Marie.

"I didn't see Elvis perform until the '68 Special. I never saw him live [before that]," Priscilla recalled in a 2017 interview. "I'm actually happier because I was able to know the man. It wasn't being interrupted by his fame, even though he was famous in Germany when I met him being only 14. I really liked him. I liked him very much."

Presley's use of prescription drugs grew while Elvis was in the army due to the stressful physical conditions he had to endure as a soldier. But as of March 1960, only time would tell what would happen in Presley's future. The King of Rock and Roll had just completed 711 days on active duty during the height of his career. All in all, it was an overwhelmingly positive experience. One reporter called Elvis "the most exalted soldier since MacArthur." Rising to the rank of sergeant in two years was a great personal accomplishment.

"I hope I got the point across that I did do the job and I don't have to take any special privileges and favors or use influence," Elvis told a reporter in 1959. "Not only to the general public, but the boys in the Army. All my life I never liked to lose."

Presley found great satisfaction in knowing that he could succeed in all the duties that the army threw at him: "I'm glad it turned out the way it did. I learned a lot. I learned that no matter how rough the duty got, I could stay with it. That meant a lot to me."

Elvis would proudly wear his army uniform onscreen in *G.I. Blues* and briefly in *Blue Hawaii* and *Kid Galahad*. Released in November 1960, *G.I. Blues* was his first movie after leaving the service. Presley's character, Tulsa McLean, just happened to be a Specialist 5 (SP5) in a tank battalion with the 3rd Armored "Spearhead" Division in West Germany. The movie would become Presley's third highest-grossing film.

As a show of appreciation to the German people, Presley recorded "Wooden Heart" for the soundtrack of *G.I. Blues*. It was based on the old German folk song "Muss i denn." The folk song, which translated into English meant "Must I, then," was a romantic farewell song that became popular among the Germany military. In his version, Elvis sang two verses in German. "Wooden Heart" was released as a single in Europe and sold two million copies in Germany. It went to number one in the U.K. and stayed there for six weeks.

"In a way, Elvis' stint in the army was a breathing period," observed Lamar Fike. "It freed him from the crushing demands of his career, and in some ways, from the needs of his family. Now he had to go home and start all over again."

"I had the feeling that he was just real happy to be a normal person again," Rex Mansfield described. "He'd had enough of that already. The army did more to help Elvis be normal than anything he ever did... You learn more about yourself, where you stand in life, in the army, than anywhere else."

Elvis mentioned to several people that if he did not already have his entertainment career, he would have stayed in the army. Years later, Presley's admiration and respect for the U.S. military and its leaders was evident in his love for the movies *Patton* (1970) and *MacArthur* (1977). In addition to memorizing parts of the *Patton* film, Elvis had also memorized General Douglas MacArthur's famous farewell speech before a joint session of Congress on April 19, 1951 which famously said "Old soldiers never die – they just fade away."

"I saw sparks of leadership in Elvis that made me think he could have induced men to follow him into combat," observed Lt. William Taylor, "just as his music caused millions of young people to follow him."

As a memento of his achievement, it was discovered that for 17 years Elvis kept a newspaper clipping about his army service in his wallet from March 1960 until the day he died in 1977. The article discussed the remarks made on March 4, 1960 by the U.S. Senator from Tennessee, Estes Kefauver, when he entered a "Tribute to Elvis Presley" into the Congressional Record praising Presley's service to the country. How ironic that Kefauver had been on the Senate Subcommittee on Juvenile Delinquency just a few years earlier. His full statement read:

"About two years ago, a young Tennessean became a member of our Armed Forces under highly publicized circumstances. I am referring to Elvis Presley, of Memphis, who is now in the process of being honorably discharged from the Army.

I have not talked to Sgt. Elvis Presley since he was inducted as a private into the service, but I presume his fame as a rock and roll singer posed a personal problem for him when he first donned a military uniform.

It may have been a temptation for him to have asked for special privileges because of his civilian fame as an entertainer. To his great credit, this young American became just another GI Joe. He went through recruit training with one intent and that was to become a good soldier. After his recruit training, the then Private Presley was assigned to an oversea unit. Here too, Private Presley concentrated on the job at hand: That of being a credit to his country as a peacetime soldier. In recognition of his service, he was promoted by his superiors to the rank of sergeant. At no time did he complain or ask for special consideration.

Some of my generation may ridicule the antics of rock 'n rollers, but none of them will find fault with Sgt. Presley or millions of other young Americans who have served and will continue to serve their country in both peace and war with both courage and patriotic zeal.

Sgt. Presley will return to his hometown of Memphis to be greeted by thousands of his neighbors in a well-deserved homecoming ceremony. I, for one, would like to say to him: 'Yours was a job well done, soldier.'"

APPENDIX A
TIMELINE OF ELVIS PRESLEY'S
ARMY SERVICE

1953

January 19: Elvis Presley registers for the draft in Memphis as required by law.

1957

January 4: Elvis gets his preinduction physical at Kennedy Veterans Hospital in Memphis.

December 20: Elvis is personally handed his induction notice by the Chairman of the Memphis Draft Board, Milton Bowers, Sr.

December 24: Elvis requests a 60-day deferment from his original induction date of January 20, 1958 so he can film *King Creole*.

1958

March 24: Elvis Presley is inducted into the U.S. Army in Memphis and later that day is sent to Fort Chaffee in Arkansas for further processing.

March 25: Elvis gets his famous G.I. haircut at the Fort Chaffee Barbershop.

March 26: Elvis is assigned to the Second Armored Division - General Patton's "Hell on Wheels" – in Fort Hood, Texas. (Rank: E-1 Trainee)

March 28: Private Presley arrives at the Fort Hood army base near Killeen, TX for eight weeks of basic training. He is assigned to Company A of the Second Medium Tank Regiment, 37th Armor of the Second Armored Division.

April/May: Elvis is named Acting Assistant Squad Leader. Elvis earned a marksman's medal with a carbine (rifle) and pistol, and then advanced to sharpshooter level for both.

May 28: Official announcement that Private Elvis Presley will be sent to Germany in September as part of the replacement for the 3rd Armored Division of the Seventh U.S. Army.

May 31: Elvis completes basic training. He is granted a two-week furlough and drives home to Memphis.

June 10: Elvis has a one-night recording session at RCA's Studio B in Nashville.

June 14: Elvis returns to Fort Hood.

June 16: Elvis begins eight weeks of Advanced Basic Training in tanks.

July 1: Elvis rents a house in Killeen, Texas for him and his family.

August 9: Elvis completes Advanced Tank Training.

August 11: Elvis starts six weeks of Basic Unit training.

August 12: Elvis returns home on emergency leave to see his mother.

August 14: Gladys Presley dies.

August 15: Funeral for Gladys Presley in Memphis.

August 24: Elvis returns to Fort Hood.

September 19: Elvis leaves Texas on a train headed to Brooklyn, New York.

September 20: Elvis is greeted by friends in Memphis as his train makes a layover stop. He is photographed kissing local girl Jane Wilbanks.

September 22: Elvis gives a press conference at the Brooklyn Army Terminal and leaves the States on the USS Randall headed towards Germany. He is photographed kissing fan Lillian Portnoy.

October 1: Elvis arrives in Bremerhaven, Germany and gets on a train headed for Friedberg.

October 2: Elvis arrives at Ray Barracks in Friedberg and gives a press conference. Elvis is initially assigned for the first few days to be a jeep driver in Company D of the 1st Medium Tank Battalion (Patton), 32nd armor of the Third Armored Division (Spearhead). (Rank: E-2 Private)

October 5: Elvis meets 16-year-old German girl, Margit Buergin.

October 6: Elvis is reassigned to the battalion's Headquarters Company as a jeep driver in the Reconnaissance or "Scout" Platoon. Elvis, Vernon, Minnie Mae, Lamar Fike and Red West check in to the Hilberts Park Hotel in Bad Nauheim.

October 23: Elvis attends a Bill Haley concert in Wiesbaden.

October 24: Elvis attends a Bill Haley concert in Mannheim.

October 27: The Presleys move to Hotel Grunewald in Bad Nauheim.

November 3: Elvis goes on training maneuvers with his unit in Grafenwoehr, located in eastern Bavaria on the Czech border.

November: Vernon meets Dee Stanley.

November 20: Elvis meets Elisabeth Stefaniak in Grafenwoehr.

November 27: Elvis is promoted to Private First Class. (Rank: E-3 / one stripe)

Mid-December: Elvis performs private concert for the staff of the Micky Bar.

December 16: Elvis returns from Grafenwoehr.

December 20: Elvis leases a BMW 507 from a dealer in Frankfurt.

December 24: Elvis starts dating Jane Wilbanks during her stay in Germany.

December 26: Elvis attends the Holiday on Ice show in Frankfurt.

Late December: Elvis takes publicity photos for the March of Dimes with young German actress, Vera Tschechowa.

<u>1959</u>

January 1: Elisabeth Stefaniak moves into a room at the Hotel Grunewald working as Presley's German fan mail secretary.

January 8: Elvis throws a 24th birthday party at his home in Bad Nauheim.

February 3: The Presleys move to a rented house at Goethestrasse 14 in Bad Nauheim.

March 2: Elvis gets a four-day pass and goes to Munich to visit Vera Tschechowa.

March 3: Elvis and Vera visit the Bavaria Film studios.

March 5: Elvis returns from Munich.

Mid-March: Elvis and his unit return for training in Grafenwoehr for two weeks.

March 26: Vernon and Elisabeth are involved in a serious car accident.

April: Elvis gives impromptu concert at private farewell party for Sgt. Ira Jones.

April: Elvis poses for publicity photos at several locations in Bad Nauheim.

April 12: The 3rd Armored Division hosts an open house at Ray Barracks.

April 14: Elvis is assigned to help relocate a WWI memorial in Steinfurth.

April 19: Elvis hosts the winners of the *Star Revue* magazine contest at his home.

June: Elvis starts dating German girl, Heli Priemel.

June 1: Elvis is promoted to Specialist 4th Class. (Rank: E-4)

June 3-9: Elvis is hospitalized for tonsilitis at the 97th General Hospital in Frankfurt.

June 12: The start of a two-week furlough for Elvis en route to Paris. He and his entourage first stay in Munich for three days.

June 16: Elvis and his entourage arrive in Paris in the early morning and stay until June 27.

June 26: Vernon attends Colonel Parker's 50th birthday party in the States. He has recently returned from Germany and will not go back until August.

July 3-5: Elvis returns to Paris for the weekend (Friday-Sunday) with Lamar, Charlie Hodge and Pat Conway.

July 15: It is announced that Elvis will be appearing on *The Frank Sinatra Show* upon his release from the army.

August 15: On the one-year anniversary of Gladys Presley's death, Elvis is spotted at Lake Gedern while on duty; he is also spotted there and at nearby lakes for the next two weeks.

August 17: Having recently arrived in Germany, producer Hal Wallis starts filming location shots for *G.I. Blues*.

August 22: Elvis welcomes Prince Abdullah of Saudi Arabia to his house for a short visit in Bad Nauheim.

September 13: Elvis meets Priscilla Beaulieu at a party at his house.

October 19: Elvis Presley's unit goes on maneuvers at the Wildflecken training area.

October 24-29: Elvis is hospitalized for the second time with tonsilitis during maneuvers at Wildflecken.

November 2: Elvis returns to maneuvers in Wildflecken for three more weeks.

November 27: Elvis begins weekly skin treatments with a South African "doctor".

December 6: Elvis begins private karate lessons at his home.

December 19: Elvis brings Priscilla to his battalion's Christmas party.

1960

January 8: Elvis is interviewed by Dick Clark over the phone on his 25th birthday. Elvis throws a birthday party at the local recreation center in Bad Nauheim.

January 12-17: Elvis travels to Paris again for the third time.

January 20: Elvis is promoted to Acting Sergeant. (Rank: E-5 / 3 stripes)

January 24: Elvis Presley's unit goes on the Operation Winter Shield maneuvers for three weeks in Grafenwoehr.

February 11: Elvis is presented with his official sergeant stripes.

February 19: Elvis receives a long and impressive Letter of Commendation from Lieutenant Colonel T.S. Jones, Commanding Officer of the 3rd Armored Division.

February 24: Elvis is presented with a Certificate of Achievement by the Commanding General of the 3rd Armored Division, Major General Frederic J. Brown.

February 29: Elvis gives interview to Peter Hopkirk of London's *Daily Express* revealing his relationship with Priscilla Beaulieu.

March 1: On his last day in Germany, the army holds a press conference for Elvis at the Enlisted Men's Club in Friedberg.

March 2: Elvis leaves Germany by plane as Priscilla is there to see him off. The plane makes a brief stop overnight in Prestwick, Scotland.

March 3: Elvis arrives in the U.S. at McGuire Air Force Base near Fort Dix, New Jersey at 7:42 am. The army holds a press conference for him.

March 5: Elvis is officially released from the army with an honorable discharge and placed on reserve status.

March 7: Elvis arrives back in Memphis in the morning and holds a press conference in the afternoon at Graceland.

1964

February 29: Elvis is officially discharged from the Army Reserve.

NOTES

Introduction

"*I would like to write a book*": Associated Press. "Elvis To Fly To U.S. Today; Priscilla Yearns For Kiss." *The Baltimore Sun*, March 2, 1960, p. 3.

"*He went in as James Dean*": Jerry Schilling quoted in Elvis Presley Enterprises and The Commercial Appeal, *Elvis Presley's Memphis.* Canada: Pediment Publishing, 2010, p. 101.

"*The next thing I knew, the wind blew*": Hodge, *Me 'n Elvis*, p. 43.

"*While Elvis and the Sergeant were lying there*": Esposito, Joe and Daniel Lombardy. *Celebrate Elvis, Volume 1,* San Francisco, CA: Newbury Press, 2007.

"*That one was real close*": Hodge, *Me 'n Elvis*, p. 43.

"*It was more like war than you might think*": Gold, Jonathan, "Elvis in the Army: Sixty Years after 'Black Monday,' Presley's Friends and Followers Recall The King's Time in Service," *Billboard* (Billboard.com), March 23, 2018.

"*I simply cannot forget the fact that Elvis chose to serve*": Taylor, Jr., *Elvis in the Army*, p. 165.

"*I believe that the months spent in Germany*": Burk and Elter, *The King in Germany 1958-1960*, p. 73.

Chapter 1

"*I'm not worried about my hair or sideburns*": Scott, Vernon, "Elvis Presley's Going to Get Hair Cut to Nub," *El Paso Herald-Post* (TX), March 2, 1957, p. 10.

"*Elvis doesn't like to fly*": Klein with Crisafulli, *Elvis My Best Man*, p. 112.

"*the celebrity wimp-out*": Brown and Broeske, *Down at the End of Lonely Street,* p. 134.

"*had decided not to enlist*": Alden, Ginger. *Elvis and Ginger: Elvis Presley's Fiancee and Last Love Finally Tells Her Story*, New York, NY: Berkley Books, 2014, p. 6.

"*It must be a nice thought to a draftee*": Hanson, *Elvis '57*, p. 200.

"*You gotta go in as a line soldier*": Brown and Broeske, *Down at the End of Lonely Street*, p. 134.

"*Dear Mamie, Will you please please be so sweet and kind*": Fried, Ellen, "VIPs in Uniform: A Look at the Military Files of the Famous and Famous-To-

Be," *Prologue Magazine* (archives.gov), Vol. 38, No. 1, Spring 2006.

"I had to hire a special security police": Mann, May. *Elvis and The Colonel*, New York, NY: Pocket Books, 1976, p. 97.

"All the time we were having a ball": Hart, Dolores, "Private Note to Elvis," *Photoplay,* August 1958, p. 103.

"My two years in the Army can't be no worse": Scott, Vernon, "Elvis Says He'll Miss 'All Them Purty Girls'," *Albany Democrat-Herald* (OR), March 15, 1958, p. 6.

"How can I conscientiously tell other mountain boys": "Was Presley's Draft Board right?" *DIG magazine*, June 1958, p. 11.

"He would have automatically gotten the extension": Brown and Broeske, *Down at the End of Lonely Street*, p. 137.

"she hoped my wife and all my children died": Levy, *Operation Elvis*, p. 16.

"The Army didn't want the problem of his celebrity": Fike, *Elvis: Truth, Myth & Beyond*, Chapter: Elvis and Uncle Sam (e-book).

"greedy, hard-hearted and nasty": Kirkley, Donald, "'Singing' Idol'? There Ain't No Such Play," *The Baltimore Sun*, February 3, 1957, p. 87.

"Overnight it was all gone": Guralnick & Jorgensen, *Elvis Day By Day*, p. 120.

Chapter 2

"There's not much difference between this": Silver, Louis. "Pvt. Elvis Begins Army Life in Sentry-Guarded Barracks", *The Commercial Appeal*, March 25, 1958, p. 8.

"Where'd you get that?": Ibid.

"I'm sorry I didn't get to see them tonight": Martin, David G. and Sandrew, Barry, Exec. Prod. *Elvis Thru The Years*. DVD. Jersey Productions: Legend Films, 2007.

"You have shown that you are an American citizen first": Vellenga, Dirk with Mick Farren. *Elvis and The Colonel*, New York, NY: Delacorte Press, 1988, p. 105.

"as when I made my first stage appearance": U.P., "PRIVATE Presley Rises and Shines," *The Knoxville News-Sentinel*, March 25, 1958, p. 15.

"Please don't cut his hair": Levy, *Operation Elvis*, p. 9.

"I'm dreading the haircut I'll get tomorrow": U.P., "It's Pvt. Presley Now!", *The Bristol Herald Courier* (TN), March 25, 1958, p. 1.

"Dear President Eisenhower, My girlfriends and I": Hparkins, "Facial Hair Friday: Presley, Presley is our cry!", *Pieces of History: National Archives blog* (prologue.blogs.archives.gov), August 17, 2012.

"Elvis' hair might not seem very important to you": Levy, *Operation Elvis*, p. 9.

"Boy, is this one a shorty": "Elvis Presley's First Army Day at Fort Chaffee
  Reception Center" via Schroer, Knorr, Hentschel, *A Date With Elvis*, p. 13.
"65 cents out of his own pocket": "Presley Forgets to Pay for Sideburns'
  Clipping", *San Antonio Express*, March 26, 1958, p. 1.
"It doesn't feel as much different": U.P., "Pvt. Presley Loses Famous
  Sideburns", *The Morning Call* (Paterson, NJ), March 26, 1958, p. 2.
"If the government wants to sell souvenir strands": Johnson, Erskine, "Some of
  Presley Past Woven into New Movie", *High Point Enterprise*, High Point,
  NC, February 17, 1957.
"for the wonderful pictures": "Elvis loses locks but forgets to pay", *The
  Commercial Appeal*, March 26, 1958, p. 1.
"I don't want to die for my country": Taylor, Jr., *Elvis in the Army*, p. xvii.

Chapter 3

"In basic, the Army force-feeds you": Presley, Elvis as told to George Riemer.
  "What Elvis Presley learned about the Army," *The Army Blue Book 1961-
  Volume 1*, New York: Military Publishing Institute, 1960, p. 188.
"We were taught how to fire the M1 Rifle": Mansfield, *Elvis The Soldier*, p. 18.
"I caught a certain amount of teasing": Barker, George. "A Measure of Peace,"
  The Nashville Tennesseean Magazine, June 29, 1958.
"Now don't ask me what time it is anymore!": Elvis Presley quoted by George
  Klein on *The Elvis Channel*, Sirius XM radio, June 26, 2015.
"flooded with girls": U.P., "Presley Still Girl-Chased", *Fort Lauderdale News*
  (FL), April 30, 1958.
"Elvis seemed to love every minute of it": Santilli, Ray, Dir. *Elvis The Missing
  Years*. DVD. Waterfall Home Entertainment: Orbital Media Limited, 2001.
"We're all proud of him": A.P., "Elvis Presley Draws Plaudits from Army",
  Marshfield News-Herald (WI), May 8, 1958.
"Oh my Lord, son": Barrett, *Once Upon A Time: Elvis and Anita*, p. 73.
"I hate to leave my mother": A.A.P., "U.S. Army Calls Tune for Elvis Presley,"
  The Sydney Morning Herald, March 26, 1958, p. 3.
"I'm going to marry you when I get back": Barrett, *Once Upon A Time: Elvis
  and Anita*, p. 99.
"He put on a brave front": Santilli, Ray, Dir. *Elvis The Missing Years*. DVD.
  Waterfall Home Entertainment: Orbital Media Limited, 2001.
"I nearly went crazy": Portis, Charles, "Elvis Visits Sick Mother: Granted
  Emergency Leave", *The Commercial Appeal*, August 13, 1958.
"Oh, my son, my son": A.P., "Death takes mother of Elvis Presley," *St. Joseph
  News-Press* (MO), August 14, 1958, p. 1.

"She's all we lived for": Dundy, Elaine. *Elvis and Gladys*, London: Pimlico, 1995, p. 324.

"I never saw a more loving relationship": Ritz, *Elvis by The Presleys*, p. 6, 11.

"Mama loved my fans": Levy, *Operation Elvis*, p. 73.

"Oh, God, everything I have is gone": Portis, Charles, "Elvis Presley tells Mother, 'Goodby, Darling,' At Grave", *The Commercial Appeal*, August 16, 1958.

"One day about a year ago I got a chance": Dolan, Kitty, "I Shared Elvis' Love", *TV and Movie Screen*, March 1959, p. 14-15, 58-60.

"She was the most wonderful mother": "Services To Be Held Today for Elvis Presley's Mother," *The Commercial Appeal*, August 15, 1958.

"From about as far back as I can remember": Jones, *Solider Boy Elvis*, p.61, 64.

Chapter 4

"It was too much!": "The Love Story He Hides …as revealed to the editor by his best girl," *Elvis in the Army*, Volume 1, No. 1, 1959, p. 54.

"We sat on the floor eating candy": Mann, May. *Elvis and The Colonel*, New York, NY: Pocket Books, 1976, p. 49.

"It was a sort of farewell to Elvis": Parsons, Louella O., "Louella's Movie-Go-'Round", *Albuquerque Journal*, Sept 23, 1958, p. 14.

"If anything happens to Elvis": Dolan, Kitty, "I Shared Elvis' Love", *TV and Movie Screen*, March 1959, p. 58.

"All of your fan club presidents flew down here": Ibid, p. 59.

"We dated all the time, in Vegas": "The Love Story He Hides …as revealed to the editor by his best girl," *Elvis in the Army*, Volume 1, No. 1, 1959, p. 54.

"At 2 a.m. we said goodnight": Mann, May. *Elvis and The Colonel*, New York, NY: Pocket Books, 1976, p. 72.

"El was so broken up after Gladys' death": Ibid, p. 56.

"Whenever Elvis talked about marriage": Ibid.

Chapter 5

"eyes were red from crying": A.P., "Presley Ships Out; Hopes to Date Bardot", *Herald and Review* (Decatur, IL), September 23, 1958, p. 12.

"We had a long layover in Memphis": Talbot, Mary K. "Veteran's Voice: Pawtucket Pfc. was an army buddy of the 'King of Rock and Roll', *The Providence Journal* (providencejournal.com), May 23, 2021.

"*I had on this white leather coat*": Elkins, Ashley, "44 Years Later, Girl Who Kissed Elvis Celebrates His Birthday," *Daily Journal* (djournal.com), January 9, 2002.

"*The Colonel had it all figured out*": Osborne and Hahn, *Elvis Like Any Other Soldier*, p. 125.

"*He looked at everyone and said 'Hello'*": Bolstad, Helen, *TV Radio Mirror*, "All at Sea with Elvis," February 1959, Vol. 51, No. 3, p. 81.

"*He sat down several times to play piano*": Ibid.

"*Charlie, you keep me from going crazy*": Hodge, *Me 'n Elvis*, p. 10.

"*The Army is apparently torn*": "Elvis: 'Bigger Than the Generals Who Watch Over Him'", *Variety*, November 5, 1958.

"*He is under more pressure than the other soldiers*": U.P.I., "Presley Plans Busy Social Life While In Germany", October 3, 1958, *The Paducah Sun*, Paducah, KY, p. 4.

Chapter 6

"*I'd like to go to Paris*": Osborne, *Elvis Word for Word*. p. 121.

"*Everybody quoted me as saying*": A.P., "Spreading Good Will in Germany, Elvis Dates Girl with Dictionary", *Wisconsin State Journal*, November 2, 1958, p. 30.

"*I've seen her about four or five times*": Ibid.

"*He is shy and rarely speaks about himself*": Schroer, *Private Presley*, p. 77.

"*He's so different*": "Elvis and the Frauleins", *LOOK*, December 23, 1958, p. 114 via Nash, *Baby Let's Play House*, p. 278

"*I have been dating this little German*": Osborne, *Elvis Word for Word*. p. 131.

"*The girl they speak of*": Barrett, *Once Upon A Time: Elvis and Anita*, p. 129.

"*I feel mad and humiliated*": WNS, "Hunt a New Hero, Girls, Elvis Is a Cad", March 16, 1959, *The Orlando Sentinel* (FL), p. 3.

"*Elvis was roaring mad*": Ibid.

Chapter 7

"*Mah Daddy is here*": Nunn, Ray, "I Don't Break Windows – says Elvis", October 1958 via Schroer, Knorr, Hentschel, *A Date with Elvis*, p. 88.

"*Germany was the best thing*": Hodge, *Me 'n Elvis*, p. 14.

"*Captain Russell just couldn't handle the situation*": "Elvis in the U.S. Army", *Witness History*, BBC World Service radio special (https://www.bbc.co.uk/programmes/w3csvtxc), March 20, 2018.

"*The assignment of scout jeep driver*": U.P.I., "Elvis Gets 'Scout' Jeep Driver Job", *The Orlando Sentinel* (FL), October 7, 1958, p. 5.

"That rumor didn't make much sense": Taylor, Jr., *Elvis in the Army*, p. 16.

"As time passed, Elvis became our friend": Jones, *Solider Boy Elvis*, p. 84.

"I'm enjoying myself in the army": King, Gilbert, "Presley: The Living Legend", *Melody Maker*, September 12, 1959, p. 2-3 via *Uncut Legends: ELVIS*, Issue no. 5, IPC Media, 2005, p, 70-71.

"I can look you straight in the eyes": Burk and Elter, *The King in Germany 1958-1960*, p. 92.

"History repeated itself": Mansfield with Terrill, *Sergeant Presley*, p. 72.

Chapter 8

"the place went nuts": Jones, *Solider Boy Elvis*, p. 120.

"My security was going crazy": Levy, *Operation Elvis*, p. 86.

"the tops were off all jeeps": Taylor, Jr., *Elvis in the Army*, p. 79-80.

"Well, Lootenet, it's funny about you": Ibid, p. 89.

"He shook everybody's hand": Culture and Military Museum Grafenwoehr, *Elvis Presley in Grafenwoehr*. DVD.

"A sergeant gave Elvis and some other G.I.s pills": Mansfield, *Sergeant Presley*, p. 123.

"He had marked up different pages": Barrett, *Once Upon A Time: Elvis and Anita*, p. 58.

"I thought I was going to faint": Mansfield, *Sergeant Presley*, p. 86.

"He had a certain way he liked his food": Gold, Jonathan, "Elvis in the Army: Sixty Years after 'Black Monday,' Presley's Friends and Followers Recall The King's Time in Service," *Billboard.com*, March 23, 2018.

"I could see how much Elvis loved and adored": Mansfield, *Sergeant Presley*, p. 88.

"When Elvis was in Germany": Ritz, *Elvis by The Presleys*, p. 16.

"I'm proud to have a stripe": U.P.I., "Elvis Presley Promoted to PFC", *The Delphos Courant* (OH), November 28, 1958.

"We hope nobody complains that Elvis was promoted": Ibid.

"during off-duty hours. Life wanted": Levy, *Operation Elvis*, p. 88.

"Do you think I look fat?": U.P.I., "Elvis was sentimental, worried about looks," *UPI Archives* (https://www.upi.com/Archives), December 1, 1986.

"That can't be. I wash my Jeep myself": Kaiser, G., "Grafenwoehr loses attraction, teen idol Elvis Presley leaving training grounds today – King of Rock and Roll in private," *Der Neue Tag*, December 16, 1958, via Heigl, *Sergeant Elvis Presley in Grafenwoehr*, p. 61.

"We think he's a great guy": Ibid, p. 60.

Chapter 9

"My grandma makes the menus": Levy, *Operation Elvis*, p. 90.
"He knew the soldiers respected him": Jones, *Solider Boy Elvis*, p. 170.
"I bet you never thought": U.P.I., "Elvis was sentimental, worried about looks," *UPI Archives* (https://www.upi.com/Archives), December 1, 1986.
"Everyone loves their mother": Osborne, *Elvis Word for Word*, p. 464.
"He did enjoy being able to talk to a girl": "Saturday Night Bash (with Elvis Presley)", *Movie Stars TV Close-ups*, Vol. 11, No. 6, June 1959, p. 32-33.
"Foghorn, the boys are going to show you": Mansfield, *Sergeant Presley*, p. 95.
"Beautiful girls were constantly coming and going": Ibid, p. 100.
"But he's my manager": Barrett, *Once Upon A Time: Elvis and Anita*, p. 126.
"Listen my Love never doubt": Osborne, *Elvis Word for Word*, p. 129.

Chapter 10

"My biggest concern was getting out of there": "The chauffeur who shared sandwiches with Elvis", *WELT* (www.welt.de), May 21, 2013.
"an unconfirmed report that Presley": A.P., "Presley Death Rumor Leaves Old Rocker Shaken", *Nashville Tennessean*, January 15, 1959, p. 21.
"These things happen": Callcott, John, "Reports Elvis Presley Was Killed Are False", *The Duncan Banner* (OK), January 15, 1959.
"The Mercedes was a total loss": Mansfield, *Sergeant Presley*, p. 114.

Chapter 11

"They had a cake and he sang": Elkins, Ashley, "44 years later, girl who kissed Elvis celebrates his birthday," *Daily Journal* (Tupelo, MS) (djournal.com), January 9, 2002.
"It was very easy for Elvis to relate to me": Long, Robert Lee, "Elvis' former girlfriend backs license plate idea", *DeSoto Times-Tribune* (desototimes.com), April 13, 2009.
"As far as Janie was concerned": Mansfield, *Sergeant Presley*, p. 100.
"She is a very well-known film star": Mallmann, Oskar, "My time as Elvis' taxi driver," *Elvis.de* (www.elvis.de), February 11, 2013.

Chapter 12

"It was just a huge, huge hit": Burns, Ken, Dir. *Country Music*, Episode 4, "I Can't Stop Loving You (1953-1963). TV mini series. Florentine Films: WETA Productions, 2019.

"Me record an Italian song?": Osborne, *Elvis Word for Word*, p. 122.

"The originators of such troubles": Schroer, Knorr and Hentschel, *A Date With Elvis*, p. 94.

"I like rock and roll because it's selling": Scott, Vernon, "Elvis Presley Himself Declares He Can't Sing," *Tampa Bay Times* (St. Petersburg, FL), June 9, 1956, p. 11.

"I enjoy rock and roll": Elvis Presley Enterprises and The Commercial Appeal, *Elvis Presley's Memphis*. Canada: Pediment Publishing, 2010, p. 28.

"He'd play a Beatles record": Nash, *Elvis and the Memphis Mafia*, Chapter 28 (e-book).

"was more of a promoter": *This Morning* (TV show), YouTube.com, November 22, 2019.

"Have just received the report": Guralnick and Jorgensen, *Elvis Day By Day*, p. 128.

"They were an unbeatable team": Guralnick, Peter, *Careless Love*, p. 4.

"One of the luckiest things": Johnson, Robert, "Chapter Five", *Elvis Presley Speaks!* magazine, 1956, p. 43.

Chapter 13

"I know that my bodyguards aren't angels": Burk and Elter, *The King in Germany 1958-1960*, p. 107.

"I am proud and honored": Schroer, Knorr and Hentschel, *A Date With Elvis*, p. 101.

"I can't imagine how": Levy, *Operation Elvis*, p. 97.

"Private Presley is being permitted to live off post": Anderson, Margaret, "Army Bows, Elvis to Bunk in a Castle", *The Des Moines Register* (IA), October 10, 1958, p. 1.

"inhospitable, dilapidated furniture": von Westrem, *Elvis and Heli*, p. 30-31.

"Phone goes all the time": Levy, *Operation Elvis*, p. 95.

"The high tip, his words 'very good'": Stein, Karl-Heinz, "My Memories of Elvis Presley", *Elvis Presley Association Bad Nauheim-Friedberg* (elvis-presley-verein-bad-nauheim-friedberg.de).

"even if only for half an hour": Burk and Elter, *The King in Germany 1958-1960*, p. 68.

"There was something different about Elvis": Abramsohn, Jennifer, "The King is Dead, Long Live the King", *Deutsche Welle* (dw.com), January 7, 2005.

"If a teenager was thought missing": "Elvis Presley specialist Claus-Kurt Ilge visits Grafenwoehr", *Onetz* (onetz.de), October 22, 2019.

"*I'd never do that*": Hazen, Cindy and Mike Freeman, *The Best of Elvis*, Memphis, TN: Memphis Explorations, 1992, p. 140.

"*Elvis was loved by all of us*": "Elvis in Bad Nauheim – A Revolution of the Hearts!", *Bad Nauheim online museum* (www.crowdfunding-bad-nauheim.de), June 7, 2015.

"*men, mature mothers with their young ones*": Schroer, Knorr and Hentschel, *A Date With Elvis*, p. 194.

"*We teenagers knew exactly when*": Ilge, Claus-Kurt, "Elvis Lives – in Friedberg", *Der Spiegel* (Spiegel.de), October 22, 2014.

"*Elvis was an idol*": Ibid.

"*He's quite normal*": "My Neighbor Elvis", *The Memphis Flash* (memphisflash.de), August 7, 2015.

"*gently strokes her cheek*": Ibid.

Chapter 14

"*because, naturally, he wanted to see Vera*": "Rendezvous in Munich: Private Elvis Presley visited Vera Tschechowa", *BRAVO*, No. 12, 1959, via Roth, The Ultimate Elvis in Munich Book, p. 56.

"*After all, he only has a few days of vacation*": "Elvis Presley in Munich", *Abendzeitung*, No. 54, March 4, 1959, via Roth, *The Ultimate Elvis in Munich Book*, p. 50.

"*The most impressive thing about him*": Holetz, Lotte, "Our little film carousel: Lotte Holetz reports from Munich", *Abendzeitung*, March 4, 1959, page 2 via Roth, *The Ultimate Elvis in Munich Book*, p. 27, 50.

"*cheap... uncouth...a gangster*": Riemer, George, "Look What Germany's Done To Elvis!", *Des Moines Register* (IA), July 19, 1959.

"*Anyone who would attend theater*": Ibid.

"*Elvis is a simple, intelligent boy*": Ibid.

"*a very low opinion of Red and Lamar*": Schroer, *Private Presley*, p. 81.

"*One of his bodyguards said*": Cortez, *Private Elvis*, p. 54.

"*Elvis was after her, all right*": Nash, *Elvis and the Memphis Mafia*, Ch. 17 (e-book).

"*That was all her mother*": Roth, *The Ultimate Elvis in Munich Book*, p. 75.

"*We hope we'll be able to make films*": Schroer, *Private Presley*, p. 90.

"*I've gotten tired of all the fantastic stuff*": Weekend (Australia), 1960 via Roth, *The Ultimate Elvis in Munich Book*, p. 75.

"*Vera sure wasn't out to use me*": Beyl, Thomas, *BRAVO*, No. 52, 1959 via Roth, *The Ultimate Elvis in Munich Book*, p. 79.

Chapter 15

"*Most people I know don't want any more*": Taylor, *Elvis in the Army*, p. 128.

"*He was sullen and disturbed*": Beagley, Piers, "Billy Smith, Elvis' cousin and Memphis Mafia member talks candidly to EIN," *Elvis Information Network* (ElvisInfoNet.com), January 2006.

"*Elvis was constantly getting demerits*": West, Bobby "Red", "His Best Friend Explodes the Lies About Elvis", *Movie Mirror*, December 1958, via *The Elvis Years 1956-1977*, No. 1, 1979, p. 104.

"*it was Elvis' ROTC days in high school*": Bradley, Don, "Elvis Was at Fort Hood for duty 55 years ago," *Odessa American* (TX), March 13, 2013, p. 5B.

"*We agreed that only one encore*": Scrivener, Mildred, "Schoolteacher Who Knew Him When Says: It's a Miracle That Elvis Is a Star", *National Enquirer*, November 1964, via *The Elvis Files Magazine*, Issue 6, December 2013, p. 42.

"*Mrs. Scrivener was responsible for urging*": Crann, Alice, "Recalling Elvis, Tender and True," *Pensacola News Journal* (FL), August 16, 1987, Section E, p. 1.

"*I might have been in uniform before this*": Fortas and Nash. *Elvis from Memphis to Hollywood*, p. 84.

"*I gotta go and I'm goin'*": Ibid.

"*I'm strictly for Stevenson*": "National Affairs: Who's for Whom", *Time* (content.time.com), September 10, 1956.

"*and I hope I never do*": "Elvis Fairly Safe (Draft, That Is!) Memphis Asserts", *Cincinnati Enquirer*, August 9, 1956, p. 11.

"*We're going to take you to Miami*": Osborne and Hahn. *Elvis Like Any Other Soldier*, p. 337.

"*I just can't leave these 40,000 men*": Ibid.

"*I never met Presley, but he had a great reputation*": Britt, Myrlen, "Lt. Taylor seemed to have his facts straight, Presley had the reputation of being a good soldier!", *Amazon.com*, Book review for Elvis in the Army by William Taylor (Amazon.com), February 12, 2016.

"*Presley was cold, he was wet*": Meiler, Olaf, "Elvis Presley as a soldier on the Grafenwoehr training area in Upper Palatinate", *Volksfest Grafenwoehr* (volksfest-grafenwoehr.de), January 11, 2005, via web.archive.org.

"*He has fooled us all*": Anderson, Omer, "Army Pleased with Elvis Presley, Officer Hopes He Will Re-Enlist", *Chattanooga Daily Times* (TN), February 15, 1959, p. 39.

Chapter 16

"raised her face and kissed the tears": Jones, *Soldier Boy Elvis*, p. 83.

"I thought the Gasthaus would explode": Taylor, Jr., *Elvis in the Army*, p. 162.

"I can't believe that you two are both leavin'": Ibid, p. 160.

"I have become accustomed to ducking fans": Jones, *Soldier Boy Elvis*, p. 249.

"We are up at a place called Grafenwoehr": Osborne, *Elvis Word for Word*, p. 130.

"You know I am bound to be pretty lonely": Ibid, p. 131.

"Eyewitness accounts (by teenage observers) are reporting": "First Field Training for Jeep Driver Presley", *Film Journal*, November 1958, via Schroer, Knorr and Hentschel, *A Date With Elvis*, p. 110.

"Most maneuvering took place around Elvis": Ibid.

"When no one was watching": Mansfield, *Elvis The Soldier*, p. 156.

"Twice he came with me to repair some jukeboxes": Culture and Military Museum Grafenwoehr, *Elvis Presley in Grafenwoehr*. DVD.

"wanted schnitzel with fried potatoes": Baumer, Ulla Britta, "Elvis Presley thanked him with an original gesture – Raimond Rodler remembers: private concert in the Micki-Bar", *Onetz* (onetz.de), October 8, 2016.

"We had breakfast together": Culture and Military Museum Grafenwoehr, *Elvis Presley in Grafenwoehr*. DVD.

"Who is the one playing so nicely?": Ibid.

"Elvis sang without a microphone": "Elvis in the Army, Part 2 – Germany", *Rex Martin's Elvis Moments in Time* (tapatalk.com), November 14, 2018.

"Afterwards, he called us two or three times": Culture and Military Museum Grafenwoehr, *Elvis Presley in Grafenwoehr*. DVD.

Chapter 17

"Most of the photos being when you are off duty": Letter from Colonel Parker to Elvis and Vernon Presley, March 23, 1959.

"It's supposed to be hush-hush": *Nashville Banner*, April 17, 1959, p. 19.

"I hated to go to breakfast with Elvis": Hillier, Bevis, "Breakfast with Elvis: Today, Don Cravens Sells Real Estate in Reseda. But as a Press Photographer, He Spent Time in Germany with Presley, and Frau Goering," *Los Angeles Times* (latimes.com), August 17, 1986.

Chapter 18

"There would be at least a couple of girls": Guralnick, *Careless Love*, p. 18.

"because of a rumor then": U.P.I., "Elvis was sentimental, worried about looks," *UPI Archives* (https://www.upi.com/Archives), December 1, 1986.

"Our friendship really surprised me": Mansfield, *Sergeant Presley*, p. 100.

"I dated Elvis just like I did other people": U.P.I., "Elvis was sentimental, worried about looks," *UPI Archives* (https://www.upi.com/Archives), December 1, 1986.

"It was an awkward position Elvis had put me in": Mansfield, *Sergeant Presley*, p. 101.

"he was going to see on a regular basis": Guralnick, *Careless Love*, p. 18.

"I couldn't believe it": Kiel, Rosemarie, "Pepsi on the pants: Winner of Star Revue-Quiz Rosemarie Kiel visits Elvis on April 19, 1959", via Schroer, Knorr and Hentschel, *A Date With Elvis*, p. 147.

"While he was talking, he laughed so much": Ibid.

"He was so sensitive and romantic": Burk and Elter, *The King in Germany 1958-1960*, p. 49, 53.

"Elvis sang some songs in German": "50 years ago Elvis Presley became a soldier in Germany – and Roswitha Klaus his girlfriend. In the BZ she tells her love story with the king of rock 'n' roll for the first time", *B.Z. Berlin* (bz-berlin.de), August 3, 2008.

"He would sit on the edge of the bed": Burk and Elter, *The King in Germany 1958-1960*, p. 53.

"'Let's go!' Elvis shouted": von Westrem, *Elvis and Heli*, p. 25.

"Elvis and I... kissed": Ibid, p. 27.

Chapter 19

"Not unless it's absolutely necessary": Elvis Presley interview with Tom Moffatt, "Uncle Sam's Man", June 1959, Audio via "Elvis In His Own Words – 1950s", *Keith Flynn's Elvis Presley Pages* (KeithFlynn.com).

"for old times sake": Roth, *The Ultimate Elvis in Munich Book*, p. 47.

"Kill the bastard": Mansfield, *Sergeant Presley*, p. 139.

"Elvis had lots of fun": A.P., "Elvis Samples Paris Night Life, Burlesque", *The Orlando Sentinel* (FL), June 17, 1959, p. 6.

"Elvis is always welcome to visit": "Hunter noted" column, Abendzeitung, June 15, 1959 via Roth, *The Ultimate Elvis in Munich Book*. p. 66.

"I was sent over here by the army": Elvis Presley interview with Hannelore Krab, "Incognito in Paris", June 15, 1959, Audio via "Elvis In His Own Words – 1950s", *Keith Flynn's Elvis Presley Pages* (KeithFlynn.com).

"the first glow of sunlight": Hodge, *Me 'n Elvis*, p. 16.

"We only went sightseeing once": Adams, David, "Freddy Bienstock: Music Publishing and Elvis Presley", *Elvis Australia* (elvis.com.au), March 8, 2020.

"You guys just use this for tips": Hodge, *Me 'n Elvis*, p. 20.

"Elvis was so much like one of the guys": Mansfield, *Sergeant Presley*, p. 143-144.

"Ah! Paris, what a city": Pouzenc, *Elvis in Paris*, p. 44.

"Tight, continental slacks, sweaters": Brown and Broeske, *Down at the End of Lonely Street*, p. 196-197.

"The Lido girls fell in love with Elvis": Hodge, *Me 'n Elvis*, p. 23.

"framed the scenes on stage": Ibid, p. 22.

"We were permitted to go backstage": Mansfield, *Sergeant Presley*, p. 146.

"We usually arrived around 4:30 am": Ibid, p. 147.

"Elvis had no compunction": Nash, *Elvis and the Memphis Mafia*, Ch. 17 (e-book).

"You wouldn't believe it": Sharp, Ken, "Freddy Bienstock & Elvis, EIN Interview", *Elvis Information Network* (elvisinfonet.com), October 2009.

"Elvis, could you do me one last big favor": Handwritten notes between Nancy Holloway and Elvis Presley via Pouzenc, *Elvis in Paris*, p. 83.

"He's someone I'll always love": Ibid, p.85.

"It wasn't the Elvis we know on records": Gray, Andy, "The Night Elvis Sang in a Paris Club," *New Musical Express*, December 4, 1959 via Pouzenc, *Elvis in Paris*, p. 78.

"I had the urge. I play quite a bit": Ibid.

"I have a lot of fans who like me rocking": Ibid.

"Elvis died when he went into the army": John Lennon at press conference at Hotel Okura in Tokyo, Japan, October 4, 1977 quoted in Keith Badman, *The Beatles Diary, Volume 2: After the Breakup, 1970-2001*, New York: Omnibus Press, 2001, p. 213.

"Elvis loved opera": Nash, *Elvis and the Memphis Mafia*, Ch. 16 (e-book).

"One more time. Up to the Arch": Hodge, *Me 'n Elvis*, p. 30.

"When he came back, [Elvis] had a program": Osborne and Hahn. *Elvis Like Any Other Soldier*, p. 202.

"There was another reason Elvis liked Paris": Nash, *Elvis and the Memphis Mafia*, Ch. 17 (e-book).

"It [Paris] reminds me so much": Buchwald, Art, "Press Conference with Elvis Presley", *New Castle News* (PA), June 26, 1959, p. 4.

Chapter 20

"*Elvis would occasionally visit with me*": Malanowski, Monsignor Thaddeus F., *Sacrifice for God and Country*, Self-published, 2011, p. 59.

"*I've talked to my chaplain lots of times*": Goff, Vivien, "Elvis' First Civilian Interview", *TV & Movie Screen*, May 1960, p. 93 via *The Elvis Years 1956-1977*, No. 1, 1979, p. 34, 93.

"*That woman is making a fool*": Barrett, *Once Upon A Time: Elvis and Anita*, p. 165.

"*He'll look like Elvis from a distance*": "3rd Armored Division Co-Stars with Elvis", *Stars and Stripes*, 1959 via *Elvis Australia* (elvis.com.au), March 25, 2005.

"*I noticed that he was not happy*": "Uncle Gustav's hut", *The Memphis Flash* (memphisflash.de), February 28, 2018.

Chapter 21

"*Small and petite, with long brown hair*": Presley, *Elvis and Me*, p. 19.

"*it was chosen for me*": Finstad, Suzanne. *Child Bride*, p. 33.

"*could make Elvis laugh so hard*": Adams, David, "Interview with Anita Wood", *Elvis Australia* (elvis.com.au), December 29, 2019.

"*was like Robin Williams*": Finstad, Suzanne. *Child Bride*, p. 88.

"*The meeting with Cliff*": Nash, *Elvis and the Memphis Mafia*, Ch. 16 (e-book).

"*He's a great artist*": Hopkins, *Elvis*, Ch. 10 (e-book), p. 144.

The court ruled in her favor: "Presley Wins Defamation Lawsuit," A.P. (apnews.com), August 25, 1998.

"*You're kidding. How do you know*": Ritz, *Elvis by The Presleys*, p. 60.

"*For a girl her age, she held her own*": Finstad, Suzanne. *Child Bride*, p. 88.

"*Priscilla did have a way about her*": Hodge, *Me 'n Elvis*, p. 45.

"*I'm looking at that picture*": *An Evening with Priscilla Presley* (live talk), Modesto, CA, January 11, 2019 via Facebook.com.

"*Baby, you don't have to worry*": Ibid.

"*And she's young enough*": Mansfield, *Sergeant Presley*, p. 154.

"*I noticed he had kind of a glazed-over look*": Mansfield, *Sergeant Presley*, p. 153-154.

"*When Elvis latched onto Priscilla*": Nash, *Elvis and the Memphis Mafia*, Ch. 17 (e-book).

"*Priscilla knew the rules*": Finstad, Suzanne. *Child Bride*, p. 89.

"*Since the weather was so bad*": Presley, *Elvis and Me*, p. 56.

"*We were in this wooden area north*": Press office, "General Colin Powell on Elvis Presley the soldier and patriot", for *The GI Blues of Elvis Presley*, BBC Radio 4 (bbc.co.uk/pressoffice), August 21, 2007.

"*One time, I got a heck of a cold*": Pepper, Grant, "60 years after serving in military with Elvis, Johnstown man honored", *Knox Pages* (knoxpages.com), October 21, 2018.

"*caught a cold and had to be*": Osborne and Hahn, *Elvis Like Any Other Soldier*, p. 201.

"*I talked with Elvis maybe once a month*": Klein, *Elvis My Best Man*, p. 124.

"*My Dearest Darling 'Little'*": Excerpts of Letter from Elvis Presley to Anita Wood, Barrett, *Once Upon A Time: Elvis and Anita*, p. 132.

"*She'd soothe him with baby talk*": Nash, *Elvis and the Memphis Mafia*, Ch. 25 (e-book).

"*I really felt I got to know who Elvis Presley was*": Guralnick, Careless Love, p. 42.

Chapter 22

"*A part of Elvis' personality*": Ritz, *Elvis by The Presleys*, p. 181.

"*Elvis was very willing to talk*": Schroer, *Private Presley*, p. 138.

"*Elvis was athletic and well-trained*": Stecker, Andreas, "Elvis and Karate", *Elvis & Karate* (crowdfunding-bad-nauheim.de).

"*He was giving Elvis a massage*": Nash, *Elvis and the Memphis Mafia*, Ch. 17 (e-book).

"*I'm going to kill the son of a bitch!*": Mansfield, *Sergeant Presley*, p. 176.

"*I noticed Elvis treated her differently*": Ibid, p. 199.

"*Rex, you know that Elisabeth*": Ibid, p. 162.

"*That Rex Mansfield is such*": Ibid, p. 162.

"*snuggle up to that little bitty thing*": Barrett, *Once Upon A Time: Elvis and Anita*, p. 130.

"*Never in the history of the orphanage*": Mansfield, *Sergeant Presley*, p. 179.

"*Elvis was a big lover of opera*": Interview with Priscilla Presley, *The Leonard Lopate Show*, October 26, 2015.

"*Cilla was dressed very simply*": Presley, Dee, Billy, Rick, and David Stanley, *Elvis We Love You Tender*, New York, NY: Delacorte Press, 1980, p. 52.

"*I'll cherish these forever*": Presley, *Elvis and Me*, p. 54.

"*We had a Christmas party here*": Elvis Presley interview with Dick Clark, January 8, 1960, Audio via "Elvis In His Own Words – 1960s", *Keith Flynn's Elvis Presley Pages* (KeithFlynn.com).

"*I saw too many drunks in my youth*": Pouzenc, *Elvis in Paris*, p. 105.

"*A very thin, healthy and bright boy*": Ibid, p. 108.

"*There was a girl he particularly liked*": "Elvis in Paris", *France Inter* (franceinter.fr), July 13, 2017.

"*This began at midnight*": Pouzenc, *Elvis in Paris*, p. 115.

"*He played with his heart and soul*": Ibid.

"*It was great!*": Ibid.

"*It was an extraordinary experience*": Ibid, p. 149.

"*It was just wonderful. I had a great time*": Neuerbourg, Hanns, "Do You Still Remember Elvis?", *The News-Palladium* (Benton Harbor, MI), October 8, 1959, p. 22.

"*He had an incredible capacity*": Schroer, *Private Presley*, p. 129.

"*The above-average achievements*": "Elvis in the Army, Part 2 – Germany", *Rex Martin's Elvis Moments in Time* (tapatalk.com/groups/elvismomentsintime) November 14, 2018.

"*Dear Mr. Seydel 'George, '*": Letter from Elvis Presley to Jurgen Seydel, Osborne and Hahn, *Elvis Like Any Other Soldier*, p. 238.

"*Elvis' whole life is singing*": Yancey, Becky and Cliff Linedecker, *My Life with Elvis*, New York, NY: Warner Books, 1977, p. 84.

"*It's a way of life*": Ibid.

Chapter 23

"*He's earned the job*": "Presley Rolls Along to Acting Sergeant", via Cortez, *Private Elvis*, p. 43.

"*designed to test our combat readiness*": Mansfield, *Sergeant Presley*, p. 188,

"*Nah. Don't want interviews*": Sparks, Fred, "Elvis Banned Interviews in Field, Lived Like Hermit While Off Duty", *Pittsburgh Press*, February 24, 1960.

"*They asked for autographs*": Talbot, Mary K. "Veteran's Voice: Pawtucket Pfc. was an army buddy of the 'King of Rock and Roll', *The Providence Journal* (providencejournal.com), May 23, 2021.

"*I had no chance myself*": Culture and Military Museum Grafenwoehr, *Elvis Presley in Grafenwoehr*. DVD.

"*He took me and put me on his lap*": Ibid.

"*reached for his coke bottle*": Text from *Neuer Tag*, February 8, 1960 via "Elvis in the Army, Part 2 – Germany", *Rex Martin's Elvis Moments in Time* (tapatalk.com/groups/elvismomentsintime), November 14, 2018.

"*He was sitting there in front of his coke*": Ibid.

"*Presley may have had mountains of money*": "King Elvis was in Hirschau 60 years ago", *Onetz* (onetz.de), February 4, 2020.

"Only a tiny proportion of draftees": Nichol, David M., "Presley and Army to Part Soon…And on the Very Best of Terms", *The Huntsville Times* (AL), February 24, 1960, p. 14.

"Your unselfish and uncomplaining attitude": Letter of Commendation from Lieutenant Colonel Jones to Elvis Presley, Osborne and Hahn, *Elvis Like Any Other Soldier*, p. 400.

Chapter 24

"There is only one reason why": Hopkirk, Peter, "Presley's Secret…It's Priscilla: Only 16 but oh so very sharp!" *The Daily Express* (London), March 1, 1960, p. 11.

"I think she's the most beautiful girl": Ibid.

"I shall be in trouble tomorrow": Ibid.

"Yes. She's about sixteen": Schroer, *Private Presley*, p. 153.

"She is very mature": Associated Press, "Presley to Leave Date, 16, Fly Home," *Lancaster Era News* (PA), March 1, 1960.

"I am very fond of him": Ibid.

"I'm too young for marriage": "Girl Friend Overseas Gets Fond Farewell from Elvis," *The Commercial Appeal*, March 2, 1960, page 3.

"He is very intelligent": Associated Press, "Elvis to fly to US today; Priscilla yearns for kiss," *The Baltimore Sun*, March 2, 1960.

"I'm not going to forget you, Cilla": Presley, *Elvis and Me*, p. 58-59.

"Little did I know": von Westrem, *Elvis and Heli*, p. 150.

"Without a long goodbye": "50 years ago Elvis Presley became a soldier in Germany – and Roswitha Klaus his girlfriend. In the BZ she tells her love story with The King of Rock'n'Roll for the first time," *Bz-Berlin.de*, August 3, 2008.

"I want you to have these": Presley, *Elvis and Me*, p. 59.

"I want you to promise me": Finstad, *Child Bride*, p. 117.

"I'll look for you from the top of the ramp": Presley, *Elvis and Me*, p. 59.

"It's all for publicity": Barrett, *Once Upon a Time: Elvis and Anita*, p. 132.

"I had read a little bit about Priscilla in the papers": Adams, David, "Interview with Anita Wood part 2", *Elvis Australia* (Elvis.com.au), June 2, 2012.

"If you've ever heard of love at first sight": Santilli, Ray, Director. *Elvis: The Missing Years*. DVD. Orbital Media Limited, 2001.

"At the [Memphis] press conference": Ritz, *Elvis by The Presleys*, p. 64.

"She has been Elvis' steady date": *The Newport Daily Express* (VT), March 5, 1960, p. 8.

"He wasn't a letter writer": Ritz, *Elvis by The Presleys*, p. 70.

"Two years passed": Ibid.

Chapter 25

"filthiest, dirtiest, back-stabbingest": Dickerson, *Colonel Tom Parker*, p. 120.

"Do I kiss you or salute you?": Ibid, p. 121.

"It's been a big help in both my career": Osborne and Hahn, *Elvis Like Any Other Soldier*, p. 485.

"Yes, I am. I mean I have my doubts": Ibid, p. 488.

"I'll probably get put in jail": Ibid, p. 401.

"I finally figured out that Elvis": Mansfield, *Sergeant Presley*, p. 211.

"Rex and Elisabeth, I urge you": Ibid, p. 230.

"It was a time of grief for me": Nash, *Baby Let's Play House*, p. 317.

"When Elvis came back from Germany": Hoedel, Sally A., *Destined To Die Young*, Williamsburg, MI: Elvis Author, LLC, 2021, p. 148.

"He now sang more from the diaphragm": Brown and Broeske. *Down at the End of Lonely Street*, p. 197.

"I wouldn't have missed it": Hopkirk, Peter, "Presley's Secret...It's Priscilla: Only 16 but oh so very sharp!" *The Daily Express* (London), March 1, 1960, p. 11.

"I want to be more of an actor": U.P.I., "Presley Begins 3-Day Chore of Becoming Civilian Again", *The Paducah Sun* (KY), March 3, 1960, p. 1.

"My dream is still to have a career": Burk and Elter. *The King in Germany 1958-1960*, p. 160.

"I didn't see Elvis perform until": *Good Morning Britain*, YouTube.com, August 16, 2017.

"the most exalted soldier since MacArthur": Levy, *Operation Elvis*, p. 83.

"I hope I got the point across": Ibid, p. 96.

"I'm glad it turned out the way it did": Halberstam, David, "Sgt. Elvis Smuggled Home in Big Fanfare of Secrecy", *The Tennessean*, March 7, 1960, p. 5.

"In a way, Elvis' stint in the army": Brown and Broeske. *Down at the End of Lonely Street*, p. 209.

"I had the feeling that he was just real happy": Gold, Jonathan, "Elvis in the Army: Sixty Years after 'Black Monday,' Presley's Friends and Followers Recall The King's Time in Service," *Billboard.com*, March 23, 2018.

"I saw sparks of leadership in Elvis": Taylor, Jr., *Elvis in the Army*, p. 166.

"About two years ago, a young Tennessean": *Congressional Record - Senate* (congress.gov), Vol. 106, Part 4, March 4, 1960, p. 4499.

SELECTED BIBLIOGRAPHY

Barrett, Jonnita Brewer. *Once Upon A Time: Elvis and Anita: Memories of My Mother*. Jackson, MS: BrewBar Publishing, 2012.

Brown, Peter Harry and Pat H. Broeske. *Down at the End of Lonely Street: The Life and Death of Elvis Presley*. New York, NY: Dutton, 1997.

Burk, Heinrich and Hans-Ulrich Elter. *The King in Germany 1958-1960*. Oldenburg, Germany: B+U Verlag, 2008.

Cortez, Diego. *Private Elvis*. Stuttgart, Germany: FEY Verlags, 1978.

Culture and Military Museum Grafenwoehr, *Elvis Presley in Grafenwoehr*. DVD. Kultur-und Militarmuseum Grafenwoehr: Panorama Videoproduktion, 2018.

Dickerson, James L. *Colonel Tom Parker: The Curious Life of Elvis Presley's Eccentric Manager*. New York, NY: Cooper Square Press, 2001.

Finstad, Suzanne. *Child Bride: The Untold Story of Priscilla Beaulieu Presley*. New York, NY: Berkley Boulevard Books, 1997.

Fike, Lamar as told to L.E. McCullough & Harold F. Eggers, Jr. *Elvis: Truth, Myth & Beyond: An Intimate Conversation with Lamar Fike, Elvis Presley's Closest Friend and Confidant*. Woodbridge, NJ: Hound Dog Books, 2016.

Fortas, Alan and Alanna Nash. *Elvis from Memphis to Hollywood*. London: Aurum Press Ltd., 2008.

Guralnick, Peter. *Careless Love: The Unmaking of Elvis Presley*. New York, NY: Little, Brown and Company, 1999.

Guralnick, Peter. *Last Train to Memphis: The Rise of Elvis Presley*. New York, NY: Little, Brown and Company, 1994.

Guralnick, Peter and Ernst Jorgensen. *Elvis Day By Day: The Definitive Record of His Life and Music*. New York, NY: The Ballantine Publishing Group, 1999.

Haeussler, Mathias. *Inventing Elvis: An American Icon in a Cold War World*. London: Bloomsbury Academic, 2021.

Hanson, Alan. *Elvis '57: The Final Fifties Tours*. Lincoln, NE: iUniverse, 2007.

Heigl, Peter. *Sergeant Elvis Presley in Grafenwoehr*. Amberg, Germany: Buch & Kunstverlag Oberpfalz, 2007.

Hodge, Charlie with Charles Goodman. *Me 'n Elvis*. Memphis, TN: Castle Books, 1984.

Hopkins, Jerry. *Elvis: The Biography*. London: Plexus Publishing Ltd, 2007.

Jones, Ira as told to Bill E. Burk. Soldier Boy Elvis. Memphis, TN: Propwash Publishing, 1992.

Klein, George with Chuck Crisafulli. *Elvis My Best Man: Radio Days, Rock 'n' Roll Nights, and My Lifelong Friendship with Elvis Presley*. New York, NY: Three Rivers Press, 2010.

Levy, Alan. *Operation Elvis*. London: Andre Deutsch Limited, 1960.

Linn, Brian McAllister. *Elvis's Army: Cold War GIs and the Atomic Battlefield*. Cambridge, MA: Harvard University Press, 2016.

Mansfield, Rex and Elisabeth. *Elvis The Soldier*. Bamberg, West Germany: Collectors Service, 1983.

Mansfield, Rex and Elisabeth with Marshall and Zoe Terrill. *Sergeant Presley: Our Untold Story of Elvis' Missing Years*. Toronto, Ontario, Canada: ECW Press, 2002.

Nash, Alanna. *Baby Let's Play House: Elvis Presley and the Women Who Loved Him*. New York: HarperCollins, 2010.

Nash, Alanna. *The Colonel: The Extraordinary Story of Colonel Tom Parker and Elvis Presley*. New York, NY: Simon and Schuster, 2003.

Nash, Alanna with Billy Smith, Marty Lacker and Lamar Fike. *Elvis and the Memphis Mafia*. Aurum Press Ltd, 2005.

Osborne, Jerry and Barbara Hahn. *Elvis Like Any Other Soldier: Special 50th Anniversary Edition Commemorating Elvis' Army Years*. Port Townsend, WA: Osborne Enterprises, 2010.

Osborne, Jerry. *Elvis Word for Word*. New York, NY: Gramercy Books, 2006.

Pouzenc, Jean-Marie. *Elvis in Paris: 60th Anniversary 1959-2019*. Paris: LMLR, 2019.

Presley, Priscilla Beaulieu with Sandra Harmon. *Elvis and Me*. New York, NY: Berkley Books, 1986.

Ritz, David (Editor). *Elvis by The Presleys: Intimate Stories from Priscilla Presley, Lisa Marie Presley, and Other Family Members*. New York, NY: Crown Archetype, 2005.

Roth, Andreas. *The Ultimate Elvis in Munich Book*. Munich: Andreas Roth, 2004.

Schroer, Andreas, Michael Knorr, Oskar Hentschel. *A Date with Elvis: Army Days Revisited*. Herten, Germany: Beluga New Media, 2004.

Schroer, Andreas. *Private Presley: The Missing Years – Elvis in Germany*. New York, NY: William Morrow and Company, Inc., 1993.

Taylor, Jr., William J. *Elvis in the Army: The King of Rock 'n' Roll as seen by an officer who served with him*. Novato, CA: Presidio Press, 1995.

von Westrem, Heli. *Elvis and Heli*. Bad Nauheim, Germany: Booy-Verlag, 2020.

Wiedemann, Dr. Peter. *Elvis Presley: The Hattsteinweiher Story*, Self-published brochure, 2017.

Young, Trina. *ELVIS Behind the Legend: Starting Truths About The King of Rock and Roll's Life, Loves, Films and Music*. Charlotte, SC: CreateSpace Independent Publishing Platform, 2015.

SPECIAL ONLINE OFFER

As a special offer to readers of this book, the author is offering free online access to additional bonus material about Elvis in the army that was not included in the book.

Please visit the book's official website at
ElvisBiography.net/ArmyOffer
to claim your free access today!

ABOUT THE AUTHOR

Trina Young is a music journalist and author of two books: *ELVIS: Behind The Legend* and *Elvis and The Beatles*.

She wrote a column about Elvis Presley for Examiner.com from 2011-2016. Her former fan magazine about The Beatles called *Daytrippin'* is now part of the permanent collection at the Rock and Roll Hall of Fame Library and Archives.

In addition to her book website, she runs an Elvis news site at https://Elvis-News.com.

Printed in Great Britain
by Amazon

15396350R00123